HISTORY OF THE
U.S. CAVALRY

HISTORY OF THE
U.S. CAVALRY

SWAFFORD JOHNSON

Smithmark

This edition published in 1994
by SMITHMARK Publishers Inc.,
16 East 32nd Street
New York, New York 10016

SMITHMARK books are available for bulk purchase for sales
promotion and premium use. For details write or telephone the
Manager of Special Sales, SMITHMARK Publishers Inc.,
16 East 32nd Street, New York, NY 10016. (212) 532-6600.

Produced by Brompton Books Corp.,
15 Sherwood Place
Greenwich, CT 06830

ISBN 0-8317-4659-9

Printed in China

10 9 8 7 6 5 4 3 2

15.99

Contents

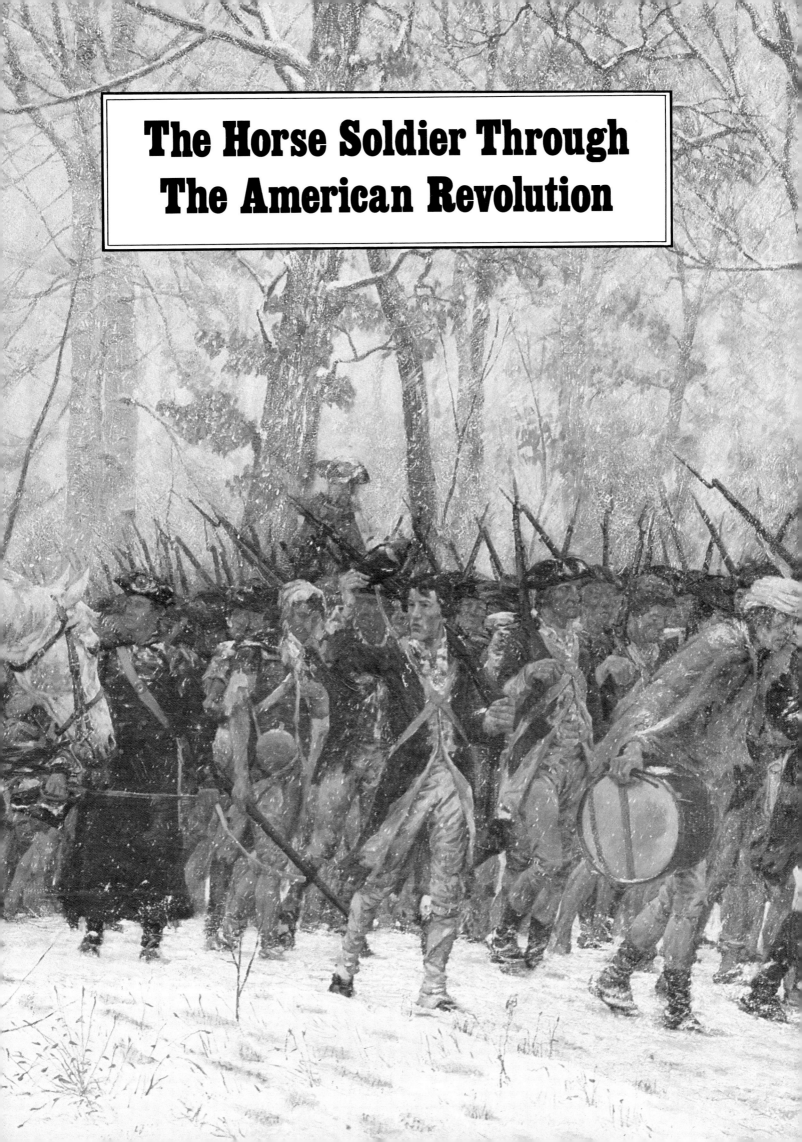

The Horse Soldier Through The American Revolution

Previous pages: *General George Washington reviewing his ragged troops at Valley Forge, Pennsylvania, in the terrible winter of 1777-8.*

Opposite, top: *In the fourth century AD, fierce Asiatic horsemen, the Huns, swept into Eastern Europe to threaten the Roman Empire.*

Opposite, bottom: *A Roman coin showing the relief of London by Emperor Constantius Chlorus, the father of Constantine (AD 285-337).*

Below: *Rameses II and his sons in battle, from the Great Temple at Abu Simbel, Egypt.*

The history of the US Cavalry should really start with that day, long before written history began, when an imaginative ancestor saw a familiar animal in a new way. That animal, the horse, was familiar to him because it was part of his food supply – our distant forebears first hunted the horse for its flesh and later took to herding the animals for both food and milk. But on the day in question, our ancestor noticed again that this creature moved a good deal faster than he did. And somehow he conceived the radical notion of climbing onto its back and gaining some of its speed for himself.

So it was that this man actually tried to jump onto the back of a horse – and found very quickly that the animal was less than enthusiastic about the idea. But he persisted, and eventually proved that a human being could ride a horse. We don't know when this happened, of course. The oldest evidence to date of man on horseback is a drawing on a bone chip from about 3000 BC, found in the Euphrates Valley. Presumably, people had been riding horses long before that and had already discovered the advantages provided in tracking other four-footed animals or pulling loads. Over the centuries, the practice spread, and as men chose the strongest and fastest horses to ride and breed, the stock improved.

It was probably not long before it became clear that the horse was useful for more than hunting and transportation – that it could also give one a significant edge in disagreements with one's fellow bipeds. The first 'combat horses' we know about, however, were not carrying mounted warriors; they were used to pull 'war carts' – probably little more than supply wagons, although some soldiers must have occasionally hopped on for a ride to the battlefield. Perhaps the oldest graphic representation of such war carts is on the Sumerian 'Royal Standard of Ur,' dated to about 2700 BC, but these rather bulky wagons, with their solid wheels, are drawn by onagers and asses. During the next thousand years or so, this unwieldy type of chariot evolved into the much lighter, swifter and more maneuverable two-wheeled chariot; its wheels,

moreover, had spokes. This type first appears among the Hurrians of North Syria, but these people may have been influenced by the nomadic, horse-culture Indo-European peoples who came off the steppes of Central Asia and Southern Russia in the years after 2000 BC. In the centuries between 2000 and 1000 BC, various peoples of that era – the Babylonians, the Hyksos, the Mycenaeans, the Egyptians, the Chinese – employed the horse-drawn chariot in warfare.

What remained was for men to combine the two traditions: horseback riding and horses in combat. Today this might seem like an obvious step, but it was not until about 1500 BC that the first mounted warriors began to appear (judging, that is, from artifacts and representations found by archaeologists in the Near East). And it is not until after 1000 BC that the mounted warrior – the true cavalryman, as opposed to individual riders who might swoop down on helpless shepherds or villagers – began to play a significant role alongside the chariot forces in battle. The leaders in this seem to have been the Assyrians, who apparently deserved their reputation as the most martial people of the ancient world. The Assyrian armies employed hundreds of thousands of foot soldiers and thousands of chariots and cavalrymen. The cavalry wore leather boots, and some wore a chain mail; they were armed with either bows or lances.

It is unfortunate that the first organized and effective cavalry force is associated with the brutal Assyrians, but ruthlessness would always characterize one type of mounted warrior – call it 'the Cossack element,' the horseman who exploits his advantage against defenseless civilians. But this is not the tradition from which the US Cavalry evolved. Instead, the US Cavalry identified with what might be called 'the Greek element' – the mounted warrior as an elite if not aristocratic member of the military. This status derived from the particular training and skills involved in fighting from a swift steed; he may or may not have been a man of wealth or leisure to acquire these skills, but his code permitted

using his mounted advantage only against armed enemies.

It was this tradition of the cavalry that led Aristotle to write: 'The earliest form of government after the abolition of kingship was one in which the citizen body was drawn exclusively from the warrior class, first represented by cavalry.' Aristotle also knew that his fourth-century BC contemporary, the Macedonian King Philip II, father of Alexander the Great, formed an elite regiment of noblemen on horseback. These riders became the most successful 'shock forces' of Philip's armies, and later of Alexander's.

Like his father, Alexander used his heavy infantry to fix his opponents, then mounted a decisive cavalry charge on the enemy's flanks to rout him. Indeed, Alexander's use of his mounted troops set the pattern for many of cavalry's classic functions through history – reconnaissance, delaying action, raid and pursuit.

These exploits of the ancients are the more remarkable when we consider that mounted warriors of those days rode bareback, often fighting with both hands and controlling the horse with their legs. The bits they used, however, were much like those of modern times: the one-piece snaffle bit dates from at least 1400 BC. Celts of the third century BC produced the curb bit, a snaffle with a chain or thong that fits along the horse's chin.

The military successes of ancient Rome were initially based almost entirely on infantry; for some time Roman cavalry was weak and poorly trained. But when the Carthaginian general Hannibal swept over the Alps with his horsemen and his elephants, the ensuing Punic Wars provided the Romans with a painful and productive lesson in the use of cavalry. The first phase of this era culminated in 216 BC with a devastating Roman defeat by Hannibal at Cannae. As always, however, the Romans were quick to learn from their enemies; in 202 BC Hannibal was defeated by his own tactics at the battle of Zama. Following this victory, Roman military strategy returned to its traditional dependence on infantry, and the cavalry arm languished. One example of the vulnerability of Roman legions to expert horse fighters came in 53 BC at the battle of Carrhae. The Roman general Crassus had taken 34,000 legionaries into the domain of the Parthians, in south-central Asia. On the plains of their country, the mounted Parthians surrounded the Roman Army, keeping well out of range of the legions' spears and swords, and rode around and around Crassus's troops, pouring a hail of arrows into his helpless infantry, mowing them down in waves where they stood. It was one of the great debacles of history.

By about AD 117 the era of Roman conquest had ended, and the Romans turned to cavalry to patrol and secure the borders of their empire. But as time went on, the barbarian hordes of

9

mounted nomads gathering around the empire became too much for Roman military might. In AD 378 Emperor Valens was routed at Adrianople by Gothic horsemen. After the fall of Rome, the power center of the West moved to the growing Byzantine Empire.

Centered in Constantinople, the Byzantines built their power on cavalry, developing a tactical system that won them victories across much of the ancient world. Byzantine mounts had shoes, saddles and stirrups. The riders were primarily heavy – that is, armored – cavalry, expertly wielding both lances and bows from horseback. To the west, another powerful force arose, also based on cavalry – the Franks. In the eighth century Charlemagne began the process of turning the Franks into expert armored horsemen to resist the depredations of the Vikings. Part and parcel of this military development was the evolution of a new social order called feudalism, as military necessity drove the peasants to bind themselves to local warlords for protection. It happened that the best kind of soldier to send against the Vikings was the mailed horseman. Thus began the long history of the mounted knight.

At the Battle of Hastings in 1066, Norman knights defeated the Anglo-Saxons, one of the great infantry hosts of western Europe. On the battlefield the horse was now supreme, and at the head of the feudal social hierarchy rode the knight. The earliest knightly armor was primarily mail, topped by a metal helmet. As the Middle Ages went on, the knight gradually became encased in heavy plate armor, his head protected by an iron pot with thin slits for eyeholes. As armor became heavier the mobility of the knight grew more restricted. Partly for that reason, all the efforts of knighthood were incapable of stopping the Mongols under Genghis Khan, whose unarmored horsemen swept across Asia and into Europe in the thirteenth century.

The Middle Ages were a time of iron men and walled towns. Both were impervious to the weapons of the day – the sword, the bow, the lance. But the arrogance of the knight and his obsession with the idealized glories of chivalry and the grand charge were not to endure. The flower of French knighthood suffered a crushing defeat at the Battle of Crécy in 1346, its charges mowed down at a distance by the newly developed longbows of the English. By that time the instrument of doom for iron men and walled towns alike – gunpowder – had already appeared. The heaviest armor could not stand up under a cannonball, or even a pistol fired at close range. In 1453 the cannons of the Turks broke down the walls of Constantinople and the city fell. With the onslaught of gunpowder weapons, cavalry declined in the 16th and early 17th centuries. But during the Thirty Years' War of the 17th century appeared the man who later earned the title 'father of modern tactics' – King Gustavus Adolphus of Sweden. His innovation was precise co-ordination of his various divisions with

Top: *The Battle of Hastings (Bayeux Tapestry).*

Above: *The Syrians at the Siege of Jerusalem (1099).*

Below: *The Sultan's Guard sounds the call to war against the infidels (Séances d'Harari, 13th-century Arab manuscript).*

Right: *Christians confront Tartars in this illustration from a mid-16th century manuscript.*

Far right: *The Horsemen of the Four Seals, armed like Saracens with crossbows and swords (Silos Apocalypse, 1109).*

Above: *A medieval miniature illuminating the initial of* Carolus Magnus, *the Frankish Emperor Charlemagne.*

Right: *Horsemen face foot soldiers in the Hundred Years' War, from the 15th-century* Chroniques de Charles VII.

full use of the benefits of new technology. He trained his cavalry carefully, using them in their traditional role of shock troops; they wielded both pistols and swords. He also organized the first regular dragoon corps, soldiers who could fight either on horseback or on foot.

In the wake of Gustavus, cavalry was revivified in the wars of Oliver Cromwell and the Duke of Marlborough in 17th-century England. Frederick the Great, King of Prussia in the mid-18th century, trained his cavalry with iron discipline; they charged as compactly as a wall and with incredible speed to ply their swords against the enemy. For a time the ancient tradition of the charging cavalryman brandishing cold steel was vindicated in battle.

By the late 18th century, European tactics had a strong resemblance to maneuvers on a parade ground. Each division of an army had its traditional functions. British military tradition dictated that the cavalry carry a heavy saber and a pair of horse pistols. Their duties were to scout, to protect the flank of the battle line, to flank the enemy, to operate against enemy communications, to pursue retreating forces and to act as shock troops. The British dragoon carried a short musket (that is, a carbine), a light sword and a pistol; he rode a fast, light horse.

When the British embarked to put down the revolution in the American colonies, they had their usual extensive complement of cavalry and

Above: *The death of King Gustavus Adolphus of Sweden in the Battle of Lutzen, 1632. His army led all Europe in the modernization of cavalry.*

Opposite: *A medieval champion of the tournament, his horse crowned with laurels (after an engraving by Albrecht Durer).*

Left: *The Emperor Maximilian I of Germany (1459-1519) taking part in a knightly tournament.*

Above: *These 16th-century Muscovy warriors with recurve bows anticipated the movement away from heavy medieval armor with their quilted padding.*

12

dragoons. As for the colonists, early successes convinced the Continental Congress that its untrained militiamen were adequate to fight the well-trained British Army. It was not until after the disastrous American defeat at Long Island in the summer of 1776 that Congress was disabused of that notion and gave General George Washington the beginnings of a regular army. As to cavalry, Washington seemed opposed at first to having any at all. Perhaps his attitude came from experience in the French and Indian War, when his British commanders had great difficulty in securing fodder, not only for cavalry animals, but for the many draft horses employed to haul wagons full of supplies and artillery.

After many bleak months for the Revolutionary cause, Washington's spectacular victories at Trenton and Princeton around Christmas 1776 gave new impetus to the war. By then Washington had a light force of dragoons, which he led himself in harassing the retreating British after the battle of Princeton. Probably he had learned something from the effective British use of the horse. But although horses served as mounts for officers and messengers, the cavalry played no role in the Revolution as fought in the northern theater.

The terrible winter of the army quartered at Valley Forge in 1777–8 is a part of American legend. Most of the stories are true – the Continentals were starving, many were unclad and unshod in the bitter cold. Nonetheless, some significant innovations were made that winter. For one, a Prussian mercenary, Baron Frederic von Steuben, began drilling the Continental Army into an efficient fighting force in the European style – though he took into account superior American marksmanship. Another historic development of that winter started when a young man of 22 named Henry Lee became a great favorite with General Washington (they were both Virginia gentlemen and related by marriage). Lee proved himself an able forager, tireless at bringing in food and fodder. In the spring of 1778, Lee was named commander of Lee's Legion, soon to be popularly called Lee's Light Horse. Lee himself gained the nickname by which he is known to history: 'Light-Horse Harry.'

Left: *The Gallic horse warrior of ancient France, who led the long fight against Viking invaders.*

Below: *Henry 'Light-Horse Harry' Lee, who fought with Washington in the Revolutionary War. His son, Robert E Lee, would carry the family military tradition into the Civil War with equal distinction.*

Throughout the war Lee's Legion was a mixture of horse and foot soldiers. He dressed them in a handsome uniform similar to that of their British counterparts, with green jackets and doeskin breeches. Though ordered to keep his horse and foot separate in battle, in practice Light-Horse Harry used them in whatever combination seemed to work best at the time. On the march he often doubled his infantry behind his horsemen. Apparently, no one attempted to teach the American cavalry the demanding drills and tactics of European-style warfare. It wouldn't have worked anyway. American horsemen did not have time to learn drill, take care of their horses and themselves, and fight too.

In the summer of 1778 Lee set out to operate against the outlying British post of Paulus (or Powles) Hook, which lay on the Hudson opposite New York City. Washington gave Lee an attacking force of 200 infantry, including a number of dismounted dragoons. Lee's detachment encountered a series of problems before they reached the fort. To begin with, they got lost. Then one Major Clark vented his anger at being commanded by Major Lee, to whom Clark was senior. After some heated words, Major Clark took half his Virginians and went home. Lee and the remaining force approached the fort waist-high in a swampy morass. A group of volunteers led the drive to tear through the fortifications; they broke straight through the outlying works and into the redoubt. Soon the British blockhouse fell, the Americans poured in

and moments later the garrison surrendered. Fifty British were wounded with bayonets and 158 were taken prisoner; the Americans lost two killed and three wounded.

But Lee's problems were not over; he and his men were still in a ticklish situation. A strong British foraging party was expected back at any moment. The Americans were exhausted, their ammunition soaked. Lugging a line of British prisoners, the detachment pushed toward an

Above: *The Battle of Monmouth, New Jersey, 28 June 1778 – an unsuccessful attempt to prevent the British from retreating to New York City.*

Opposite, top: *The Battle of Bunker Hill, outside Boston, cost the British 1150 men to the colonists' 441. The British won, but learned here that the Americans would not be easily subdued.*

Opposite, below: *George Washington takes command of the Continental Army at Boston on 3 July 1775, two weeks after the defeat at Bunker Hill. Washington made comparatively little use of cavalry, but his cousin, Colonel William Washington, was a notable leader of mounted troops.*

expected rendezvous with some boats on the river. They arrived to find the boats gone – the person in charge had grown tired of waiting. Lee's men walked home with their prisoners. During the march some of the Virginians who had left before the assault reappeared, just in time to throw back an attack by the British foraging party. It had been a spectacular, if peripatetic, operation; soon Lee's name was famous among Patriots and Tories alike. (However, his tiff with Major Clark was not over. Clark brought a court-martial against Lee, who at length was aquitted with high honors.) If the whole affair sounds like a comedy of errors somehow saved for the Americans by sheer luck and pluck, it is in that respect not unlike many American efforts in the Revolution.

The spring of 1780 found the Continental Army in desperate straits again. As always, many of Washington's troops were militia under short enlistments: when their terms were up, the militia invariably went home, even if a battle were imminent. Those soldiers remaining to Washington were on the verge of mutiny. Learning of this, British commander Henry Clinton decided to make a show of strength. He sent General Wilhelm von Knyphausen and 5000 men toward the American camps at Morristown, New Jersey. Finding a strong militia force obstructing his way across the Rahway River, Knyphausen decided discretion was the better part of valor and withdrew back into New Jersey. Washington sent General Nathanael Greene and 1000 Continentals plus a force of

militia toward the British. Harry Lee and others were directed to delay the enemy march while Greene made ready to meet the British at Springfield. Approaching the town, Knyphausen divided his forces, sending half to confront Greene and the others around the right toward the Vauxhall Bridge, to flank the Americans.

At the bridge the British ran into Lee's cavalry and a Continental regiment. After heavy fighting the Americans were driven back, but, reinforced by Greene, they made another stand on the Vauxhall Road. The Continental foot charged, bayonets on the British, and routed them. When the enemy began to fall back, Harry Lee led his horsemen to the charge, brandishing their sabers. It was a classic cavalry maneuver. A fleeing footsoldier presents his back to the sabers of enemy cavalry – a heady experience for the horseman, and almost the only time a saber is useful. On the Vauxhall Road Lee and his men made the most of it.

Unable to make headway with either of his detachments, Knyphausen decided the Americans were by no means mutinous and called it quits, withdrawing his army deeper into New Jersey. Harry Lee had won the day at the Battle of Morristown. Directly afterward, Washington made the young man a lieutenant colonel and sent him to the South, where his talents were desperately needed.

By the autumn of 1780, Revolutionary fortunes in the North, while unsteady, were at least tending toward progress. In the South, things were outright disastrous, due to a series of inept commanding generals. Asked by the Continental Congress to name a successor to General Horatio Gates, the most recent failure, Washington immediately appointed his old right-hand man Nathanael Greene. It was to prove one of the wisest things Washington ever did.

The army with which Greene was expected to conquer the South consisted of a pathetic force of 90 cavalrymen (under George Washington's second cousin, Colonel William Washington), 60 artillerists, and 1482 infantrymen, of whom a third were unreliable militia. Fewer than 800 of the whole army were properly clothed and outfitted. In January 1781 Greene reported that 'The appearance of the troops was wretched beyond description, and their distress, on account of provisions, was little less than their suffering for want of clothing and other necessaries.' Seeing that he could not hope to take the offensive, Greene decided on a daring gamble: he would divide his small forces. This would make foraging easier and force General Charles Cornwallis, the British commander in the South, to follow suit. Greene gave one of his divisions to General Dan Morgan, a hard-fighting leader from the Northern campaigns, and himself remained with the other wing. With Morgan went the cavalry of William Washington, ordered to operate between the Broad and Pacolet Rivers in South Carolina. Soon Light-Horse Harry joined Greene. Lee's Legion then numbered a little less

than 300 men, of whom only about a third were mounted. But they counted for much more than their numbers. Now old hands at harassing the British, they were experienced fighters led by a superb commander, and their mounts were in excellent shape. Almost alone in Greene's army, they were ready and able to fight.

Greene forthwith sent the Legion to take Georgetown, South Carolina. Lee was to combine forces with another cavalryman who was already becoming a legend – Francis Marion, 'the Swamp Fox.' Marion was in his mid-40s, a veteran of Indian fighting in the South. He had taken part in the frustrating and ultimately unsuccessful operations on Charleston and Savannah early in the war. Despairing of more conventional tactics, Marion had joined a group of mounted marauders who moved in and out of the swamps to harass the British. As a guerrilla fighter, the grizzled Marion found his true field of genius. His irregulars buzzed around the British like gadflys, coming out of the swamps to harass their garrisons and operations – thus the nickname given to Marion by his enemies. After their raids his men exchanged their swords for rakes and hoes and went home to play the part of innocent farmers. The British were enraged at such tactics, but could do nothing about them.

Marion's chief opponent was Cornwallis's cavalry commander, General Banastre Tarleton, a dashing, fearless and ruthless leader. At the Waxhaws, South Carolina, in May 1780, Tarleton and his men had slaughtered surrendered American troops. This made him one of the most hated men in the British Army; thereafter the

Below: *General Nathanael Greene, a gifted leader who made the best possible use of his meager resources.*

phrase 'Tarleton's quarter' was a euphemism for the slaughter of helpless captives.

A familiar – and probably fictitious – story about Marion was that of a young British officer, sent under truce to discuss prisoner exchanges, who was invited by Marion to dine with the American irregulars. Having been offered only a few roasted potatoes on a slab of bark, the Briton complained of the scant fare. Marion replied that in fact this was better than their usual ration because they had a guest. The officer, the legend concludes, returned to report to his commander that such men could not be conquered. A more likely story has it that a British major, disgusted at the ungentlemanly hit-and-run tactics of the Swamp Fox, challenged him to a cavalry duel. Marion responded that he would be glad to oblige, 20 men for 20 men. At that point the enemy commander, who had counted on his numerical superiority, withdrew the challenge.

When Harry Lee joined Francis Marion for the operation on Georgetown ordered by General Greene, it was a union of two leaders already famous among their countrymen. But like two prima donnas, each felt unhappy about sharing the command and the spotlight. Though they captured the British commander of Georgetown, they were unable to breach the fort.

Meanwhile, Cornwallis pondered his response to Greene's astonishing strategy of dividing forces. At length the British commander decided to divide his army into three parts: one was to secure Camden, South Carolina; a second, under Tarleton, was to attack Morgan's division; and the third was to move to North Carolina to mop up after the expected American defeat. The stage was set for one of the crucial battles of the Revolution – Cowpens.

Learning of Tarleton's approach, Dan Morgan decided to gamble and make a stand in front of the Broad River. His plan of battle was most ingenious. In his front he placed a division of sharpshooters who were instructed to aim for the enemy officers and then to retire, firing as they went, to the second battle line. This line, the unsteady militia, were entreated to get off a couple of shots at the British before retreating. The third American line consisted of Continental regulars situated on higher ground. Behind them and over another rise was the reserve force, mostly William Washington's cavalry. Both Morgan and Tarleton commanded about the same number of effectives – some 1100.

At midmorning of 17 January 1781, Tarleton's forces approached the waiting Americans in proper British parade-ground style. They advanced toward the first thin ranks of American sharpshooters, expecting to brush them away easily. But at 50 yards the sharpshooters fired their first volley and unhorsed 15 British officers before retiring. Tarleton ordered his dragoons to attack; they refused to advance in the face of the accurate enemy fire. Infuriated, Tarleton ordered his infantry forward. These ran into the guns of both the sharpshooters and the militia; the latter got off their two shots and retired in good order. Having already suffered heavy casualties, the British infantry pressed doggedly on while Tarleton's dragoons closed in on the apparently fleeing militia. But the dragoons in turn found

Below left: Baron von Steuben drilling Washington's army at Valley Forge, in a painting by Edwin Abbey.

Below: Washington reviewing the Western Army at Fort Cumberland, Maryland.

An old mill beside Gowanus Creek is the center of hard fighting during the Battle of Long Island, which helped save the main American army in Brooklyn Heights.

themselves attacked by William Washington's horsemen, who had appeared from behind the rise. Swords in hand, the American cavalry routed the British dragoons. Tarleton could scarcely believe his eyes.

Meanwhile, in the middle the British infantry had run afoul of the Continental regulars in the American third line. The regulars stood fast, kneeling and firing low. When Tarleton sent reserves around their right flank, the Continentals pulled back to a stronger position. By this point William Washington's horse had advanced well ahead of their infantry line. There Washington noticed the confusion of the enemy attack and sent word to Morgan, 'They're coming on like a mob. Give them one fire, and I'll charge them.' Morgan shouted to his Continentals, 'Face about, give them one fire, and the day is ours!' The advancing British saw the American line wheel and shoot. Then the Americans surged forward to attack the British with the bayonet, while Washington's cavalry assaulted them from the rear. The British line fell to pieces.

The battle ended with a remarkable incident. Washington's horsemen took out after Tarleton, who was fleeing with 140 of his dragoons. Getting ahead of his men, Washington found himself suddenly confronted by Tarleton himself. For one of the few times in any war, two opposing commanders duelled with sabers on horseback. Finally Tarleton got off a pistol shot, wounding Washington's horse, and got away.

It was a devastating blow to the British; they had lost 100 killed, 39 of them officers, and over 600 prisoners – nine-tenths of their whole force. American losses were 12 killed and 60 wounded. In a battle of almost equal forces, the Americans had bested the British at their own game, with their own infantry and cavalry tactics.

Cornwallis, hearing of the defeat, vowed to catch Greene at all costs; he prepared to move his army quickly, burning much of its supplies. Not wanting to risk a standup battle, Greene determined to lure Cornwallis north, drawing the British through North Carolina toward Virginia, farther into hostile territory. The American army pulled off to the north, Cornwallis in close pursuit. Lee, Washington and the American horse screened the army, playing cat-and-mouse with the British. It was a dangerous game indeed, but Greene believed he could outrun the British. By the time Lee reached the banks of the Dan River on 13 February, most of the American army had crossed into Virginia. The Legion's shout of victory was loud enough to be heard by the pursuing British, who realized they had lost the race.

Lee's men were the last over into Virginia. Cornwallis had chased Greene out of the Carolinas, but could not continue to pursue him – the British had no boats, and a crossing would be too risky. Neither could they remain in hostile territory that had been eaten clean by the enemy. The dejected British marched back to Hillsboro, North Carolina. In Britain, Horace Walpole aptly summarized the fruits of Greene's strategy: 'Lord Cornwallis has conquered his troops out of shoes and provisions and himself out of troops.'

Left: *British soldiers climb the Palisades from the Hudson River to Fort Lee, New Jersey, in the war's second year.*

Below: *An idealized portrait of the famous 'Swamp Fox,' General Francis Marion, in action, from a painting by Alonzo Chappel.*

On 18 February Greene sent Lee's Legion and some infantry across the river to harass Cornwallis. Light-Horse Harry got wind of a band of 400 Tory cavalry who were on their way to join the British. Moving forward, the Americans ran into two civilians who mistook them for Tarleton's cavalry – so similar were their uniforms. Lee sent the civilians ahead to tell the Tories to stand aside for Tarleton's division. Soon Lee's Legion was riding grandly past the admiring Tories. As Lee came even with the commander, Tories on the other end caught sight of the American infantry. Realizing their mistake, the end of the Tory line opened fire. Lee's men wheeled their horses and pitched into the Tories with both sabers and pistols fired at point-blank range. The Tories never had a chance: 90 were killed, many others wounded. Lee had no casualties.

In February Cornwallis marched his army southwest across the Haw River, shadowed by Lee's Legion, Washington's cavalry and 300 backwoods riflemen. Greene led his men back into North Carolina, where the opposing forces maneuvered, looking for an opening. On the morning of 6 March, Cornwallis made a move toward Greene's army but Greene was not yet ready to fight. While the rest of the American army pulled away toward a ford called Reedy Fork, the forces of Lee and Washington slowed the British van. Tarleton's cavalry slipped past the American horse and raced them to the ford, where both sides arrived almost simultaneously. With infantry reinforcement, Lee tangled with Tarleton and covered the main body's

Right: *A Revolutionary recruitment poster offering volunteers 'sixty dollars a year in gold and silver money' plus 'a large and ample ration of provisions' that did not always materialize.*

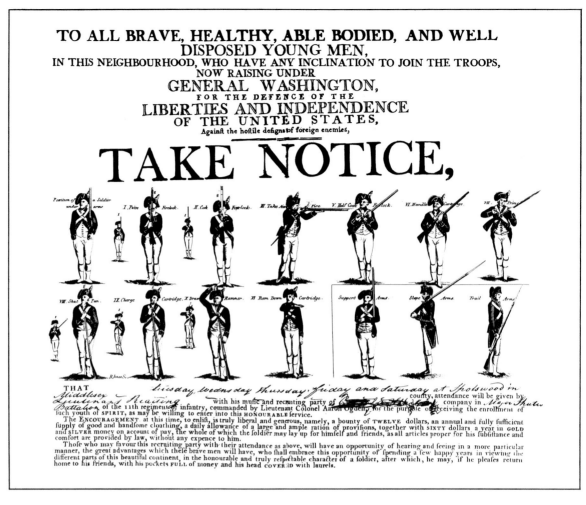

crossing. Lee, Washington and their infantry crossed last, with the British right behind them. Then Lee deployed his men to resist the British crossing. Despite the galling fire, the British maintained enough momentum to cross the stream and dislodge the Americans, whom they pursued for five more miles before giving up. It was another close call for Greene; Lee's delaying action had saved the army again.

Over the next two weeks, Greene's army, encamped at Guilford, was strengthened by some 4000 reinforcements, to the point where it could stand up to Cornwallis. Choosing his battleground carefully, Greene decided to let the enemy come to him. He sent Lee to draw them out. On 15 March Lee found Tarleton's horsemen leading the British van. After a charge that sent Tarleton scurrying back, the Legion sped back to inform Greene and join the battle lines at Guilford.

As Dan Morgan (now retired) had advised him, Greene formed his line much as it had been at Cowpens – militia in the middle, surrounded and backed by regulars, with the militia ordered to squeeze off two shots before they ran. In front of the Americans were 500 yards of open ground. The troops of Light-Horse Harry and William Washington supported the flanks. The British infantry appeared, advancing in a firm front, drums and fifes playing. Suddenly a thousand American guns spoke at once. The British line staggered on, then stopped: it faced a long line of

Continentals resting their guns on a fence and coolly taking aim. For a few moments both armies stared across a silent space. Then the British commander rode up and shouted 'Come, my brave Fusiliers!,' and his men pushed forward. Part of the British line engaged Lee's horse and foot, drifting into a private battle of their own on one side. As Lee and the British fought it out from tree to tree, the rest of the two armies, locked in close and bloody combat, muddled in the center. Perhaps Greene knew that he could call on his cavalry to rout the British, as Morgan had done at Cowpens. But Greene was averse to gambling with his whole army, which was now the best hope the Revolution had. In midafternoon he decided to retreat. As he did so, Lee's Legion kept up its fight on the side until Tarleton's horsemen arrived and sent them on their way.

The British had won the field at Guilford, but their casualties were so severe – a quarter of their army – that they were worse off than ever. Cornwallis took his devastated army back toward Wilmington, harassed constantly by Lee's Legion, which prevented British foraging during the 200-mile trek. The British arrived in Wilmington on 7 April. Learning that Greene was marching toward Lord Rawdon's army in South Carolina, Cornwallis decided he'd had enough. He resigned Rawdon to his fate and slipped into Virginia after the Americans left.

Light-Horse Harry was ordered south to re-

Above: *The death of Count Casimir Pulaski while charging the British at the Siege of Savannah in 1779. Pulaski, a Polish exile, raised a legion that bore his name for the American cause and served under General Benjamin Lincoln.*

Top right: *An encampment of General Francis Marion's guerrilla force, which prevented Cornwallis from taking control of South Carolina in the war's final stages.*

join the Swamp Fox for operations against a string of British forts in South Carolina. This time the two put aside their jealousies and worked well together. Their combined forces easily took Fort Watson, on the Santee River below Camden, on 22 April. Rawdon's communications line was severed.

Meanwhile, Rawdon himself was busy. On 25 April, at Hobkirk's Hill near Camden, his army fell upon Greene, pushing back the American line. Greene sent 60 of William Washington's horse around the perimeter to attack the British rear. Inexplicably, Washington dallied in the woods to round up a number of British noncombatants; thus he arrived after the American infantry had been routed. If much of the blame for the loss at Hobkirk's Hill lay with Washington, it remained another hollow victory for the British, who had suffered 258 casualties. American losses were 18 killed, 108 wounded, 136 missing (as usual, most of the latter were militia). After Hobkirk's Hill Greene wrote, 'We fight, get beat, rise and fight again.' The fact that Greene never won a decisive battle in his whole Southern campaign is perhaps a blot on his record, but nonetheless he remains in history as a great general, perhaps the greatest of the Revolution. At this point, with his tattered and tiny army, he was about to sweep the British out of the interior South altogether.

Rawdon evacuated Camden on 10 May. Two days before, Marion and Lee had besieged Fort

Motte, a key link in the British supply line between Charleston and Camden. Its main constituent was a mansion owned by a Mrs Motte, who cheerfully consented to the Americans burning out the British. The mansion in flames, the British surrendered, and Mrs Motte spread a bounteous dinner for both American and British officers while the captured British put out the fire. Greene and the rest of the Continental Army arrived at the fort and ordered a division of Marion's to attack Georgetown on the coast; Lee was to take on Fort Granby, the next in the British line of garrisons. At Granby, Lee exercised his wiles rather than his troops. Learning that the garrison's commander was an avaricious type, Lee sent word that the occupants could keep whatever plunder they had if the fort surrendered. The commander complied immediately.

There now remained only four British garrisons in the Carolinas – Savannah, Charleston, a fort called Ninety-Six and Georgetown. Marion's reputation had grown to the point that Georgetown hastened to surrender as soon as he arrived. Lee and his Legion moved first toward the last enemy garrison in Georgia, at Augusta. They marched nearly a hundred miles in three days, with dragoons and infantry alternating on horseback. Before reaching Augusta, Lee detoured to take a large supply of stores at Fort Galphin on 21 May. There he sent his men to make a sham attack on one side of the fort, then withdrew them and, when the enemy emerged to pursue, marched his main body right in on the other side. At Augusta Lee first captured the smaller of two forts, Grierson, then invested Fort Cornwallis, which fell on 4 June with a force of 250 Tory militia and 300 Creek Indians. With Augusta secured, Lee hurried to aid Greene, who was then besieging Ninety-Six.

The Legion arrived at Ninety-Six on 8 June. Lee found the situation a stalemate; the fort was holding fast despite all American efforts. Immediately Lee noticed that a stream and a small covered way behind the fort provided its only water: this section, neglected so far by the Americans, was the weakest part of its defenses. At Lee's direction that side of the fort was invested and the garrison's water cut off. By 17 June the British within were thirsty indeed. But that day a Tory messenger made it into the fort; a cheer from inside told Greene's army that Rawdon was approaching. After a futile assault, Greene marched his army away on 20 June. Had Lee arrived a little earlier, the fort would surely have fallen.

Rawdon pursued Greene for a while, returned to Ninety-Six, and finally evacuated the garrison, the last British stronghold in the interior South. Once again, General Greene had lost a battle but won his point. He rested his army for six weeks and gained reinforcements. Learning that a demoralized Lord Rawdon had sailed for England and his successor, Stuart, held an army at Eutaw Springs, Greene decided to take the offensive and marched his army forward. Lee, Marion and William Washington buzzed around the British as usual, denying them forage and intelligence.

On 8 September 1781, Lee and some infantry surprised a party of British digging for sweet potatoes and inflicted heavy casualties. Soon the two armies were fighting it out at Eutaw Springs. Using tactics much as at Cowpens and Guilford, Greene put his militia in the center, with cavalry under Lee and Wade Hampton (grandfather of the Confederate cavalry leader of the same name) on his flanks. Among the reserve were William Washington's cavalry. The battle raged in thick woods, the American militia fighting, for a change, like professionals. As the Americans pressed in on the center, Lee and Hampton fought their own battles on the flanks. Finally, a British surge in the center broke through the American front line, but soon came up against a strong second line. By that time the American flanks had fought their way around the British. On the British right, the fighting was so close that some opposing soldiers fell transfixed by each other's bayonets. At length, pressed on front and flanks, the British line fell back in confusion. Greene then attempted to use William Washington's cavalry in classic fashion – to turn a retreat into a rout by riding on the enemy flank. But Washington ran into a thicket, and while he was picking his way through, the British center firmed up. Emerging from the thicket and leading his men toward an opening in the enemy rear, Washington found himself under heavy flanking fire. Washington's horse went down; he was wounded by a bayonet and captured. Before reinforcements arrived, half his men were killed or wounded.

The British right was driven back to higher ground, where they mounted determined resistance under Major Marjoribanks. The rest retreated through their camps, some making a stand in a brick house. The pursuing Continentals could not resist stopping to sample food and rum left in the enemy camps, so most of the victorious Americans were soon roaring drunk. Lee took his still-sober Legion and besieged the British in the brick house. Using captured soldiers as shields, they fought their way up to the door. But Marjoribanks's infantry, still holding out on the right, turned back virtually the whole American Army and somehow emerged to drive Lee away from the house.

The day ended with the return to camp of the main British Army. At that point both armies had fought themselves to exhaustion. Greene withdrew his forces, leaving the field, and technically the victory, to the British. Losses were heavy on both sides. Only two of Greene's regimental commanders were unharmed (one being Light-Horse Harry); a quarter of his men were casualties. British losses were two-fifths of their strength; the gallant Marjoribanks was among the dead. Significantly, however, after the battle at Eutaw Springs Greene reported only eight men missing, while Stuart had 400 deserters – in other words, the British were beginning to behave like a beaten army.

There was little fighting left to do for Greene's command. On 19 October 1781, the tide turned once and for all: Cornwallis surrendered to George Washington at Yorktown, Virginia. Still the war dragged on for month after month, with the Americans mopping up here and there, until the British gave up and sailed for home in December 1783.

Light-Horse Harry Lee retired to Virginia, helped write the Constitution, served in Congress, became governor of his state and wrote his masterful *Memoirs*. When he was 50 years old, his wife gave birth to a son named Robert E Lee, who would also become a soldier of considerable distinction. Francis Marion, 'the Swamp Fox,' went back to farming, served as a state senator, and in 1784 was given command of a fort in Charleston Harbor. He died in 1795.

Admittedly, the role of American cavalry in the Revolution was small, however courageous. Throughout, Lee commanded mixed forces of horse and foot. His men fought sometimes as mounted cavalry, sometimes as dragoons, occasionally more or less as infantry. As would often be the case in American battles, the distinction between dragoons and cavalry was hazy. In a long march, Lee was not averse to doubling up on horseback, or to dismounting his horsemen and putting his weary infantry in their places. Marion usually commanded mounted forces exclusively. Neither of these men learned his tactics from tradition. Both were pragmatists, doing whatever seemed to work best for the problem at hand. Even though there was to be no established cavalry in the tiny post-Revolutionary army, an important tradition may have been established during the Revolution for future American cavalry – which was exactly that pragmatic approach to fighting.

Above: *William Washington's troops overwhelm Tarleton's Legion in the Battle of Cowpens, which ended with a saber duel between the two commanders, both of whom survived to fight again.*

Opposite: *The Battle of Eutaw Springs, North Carolina, 8 September 1781, after which the British had 400 deserters. Their breakdown of morale was completed by Cornwallis's surrender the following month.*

War and Peace in the West

After the Revolution there was no established cavalry unit in the United States for 50 years. Any mounted units that saw action were assembled for a particular emergency and then dissolved. The reasons for this policy were many. For one thing, there was the deep-rooted American fear that a standing army was a threat to liberty; perhaps cavalry, traditionally the most prestigious branch of service, represented the greatest threat. Beyond that, American leaders expected problems from overseas, or from the Spaniards in Florida or the British in Canada; none of these seemed a likely field of action for horsemen. In fact, not until the Civil War would mounted soldiers attain their full stature in the United States. Nonetheless, in the panorama of small wars and domestic tensions between the Revolution and the Civil War, the mounted units of the American armed services were to secure the cavalry a place and provide it with experience. Above all, it gradually became clear that only men on horseback could contend with the greatest threat to the young nation's unquenchable thirst for expansion – the great mass of native Americans, whom Columbus had long before misnamed Indians.

In 1792 General 'Mad' Anthony Wayne defeated a confederation of Indians at Fallen Timbers and pursued the fleeing enemy with a detachment of frontiersmen on horseback. In 1811 the Shawnees rose up under their great leader Tecumseh. Sent to deal with this threat, General – later President – William Henry Harrison summed up his adversary as 'one of those uncommon geniuses which spring up occasionally to produce revolutions and overturn the established order of things.' The 'established order' in question was the white man's right to any Indian lands he wanted; the Indians, after all, were considered ignorant and godless savages. And for all Tecumseh's brilliance and strength of leadership – he forged some unprecedented alliances among Indian tribes – he still went down to defeat before Harrison's mounted militiamen at Tippecanoe in 1811. During the War of 1812, Tecumseh was defeated again at the Battle of the Thames, between lakes Erie and Huron, where he was allied with British and Canadian troops. All were routed, and Tecumseh was killed, by a charge of mounted Kentuckians under Harrison.

After the War of 1812, no regular mounted unit remained in the tiny US Army. But as numerous settlers pushed into the Western frontier in succeeding decades, their need for protection grew. Finally, in 1832, Congress authorized a battalion of Mounted Rangers to guard the route from Independence, Missouri, to Santa Fe – the legendary Santa Fe Trail, which stretched through the territory of the Shawnee, Arapaho, Comanche, and several other formidable tribes. Before the Rangers were dispatched, the trail had been guarded by infantry, but it soon became clear that only men on horseback could match the Indians in mobility and range of

Previous pages: *The Battle of Churubusco, Mexico, during the Mexican War of 1846-8.*

Above: *American officers of the War of 1812.*

Opposite: *A Currier and Ives lithograph depicting the death of the Shawnee chief Tecumseh at the Battle of the Thames, October 1813.*

Left: *The Seminole chieftain Osceola, in a portrait by George Catlin.*

operations. The Mounted Rangers were an elite regiment, enlisted for one year; in fact, the outfit only lasted a year. That was long enough, though, to demonstrate their effectiveness and to make them harbingers of the birth of the US Cavalry. In the brief Black Hawk War of mid-1832, however, mounted militia contributed little to putting down an Indian uprising in Illinois led by Chief Black Hawk. (A group of mounted miners under Major Henry Dodge proved more successful.)

On 2 March 1833, Congress merged the Rangers with the First Regiment of Dragoons to produce the nation's first true cavalry outfit – although the nomenclature remained as hazy as ever. (Technically speaking, a dragoon usually fights dismounted, a cavalryman mounted. In fact, the US Dragoons usually fought mounted on the prairie; the first cavalry regiments so named, established just before the Civil War, were to find their greatest success in fighting dismounted.) The Dragoon regiment was commanded by the newly promoted Colonel Henry Dodge. Its lieutenant colonel, Stephen Watts Kearny, would achieve notoriety, as would a young lieutenant named Philip St George Cooke. Their stated duty was to keep the Indians peaceful over 1000 miles of frontier.

After a few months of enlistment efforts, barracks and stable building, horse collecting, and drill, the Dragoons were ready for their first expedition by June 1834. On the 15th of that month they set out from Fort Gibson, Arkansas Territory, led by Colonel Dodge (Kearny was away on recruiting duty). The 500 new troopers, most of them more conversant with Eastern streets than with Western plains, were grandly – and inefficiently – uniformed in double-breasted blue coats bristling with buttons, caps bedizened with gold cord and pompons, ankle boots, spurs and blue-grey trousers with a yellow stripe on the outside seam. (From then on US Cavalrymen would be called Yellowlegs.) The purpose of the Dodge expedition was to awe those Indians who had never been brought under government control, specifically the Comanches and Pawnee. The villages of the two tribes lay some 250 miles to the west. Another purpose was to look for a lad named Matthew Martin, who had been abducted by Indians the previous year. With the column rode two girls from the Pawnee and Kiowa, to be returned to their families. Along for the ride was Indian painter George Catlin.

The expedition set out in temperatures of 105 degrees Fahrenheit, an ominous indication of difficulties to come. Leading the way was a collection of Indian guides from the Seneca, Osage, Cherokee and Delaware tribes. Beginning a US Cavalry tradition, the column was grouped in order of the mounts' colors – whites, blacks, sorrels, bays and so forth. Wagons full of supplies, provisions and ammunition creaked along behind, followed by 70 head of cattle. Thus

Dodge set out with a confident and well-outfitted expedition – but its primary enemy would prove to be the land, not the Indians.

Within 80 miles the Dragoons were already beset with fever, dysentery, sunstroke and heat exhaustion, their horses hungry and staggering with the heat. The greenhorns were getting their first lessons in fighting in the West. On 25 June the ailing column caught up with General Henry Leavenworth, commander of the Army's Western Department. The dragoons pushed on with the general, leaving 27 sick men behind. Several days later Leavenworth and a few dragoons took out after some buffalo. The general's horse stumbled and threw him; thereafter he came down with a fever that proved fatal. By that time few Dragoons were in very good shape, either. In their stifling uniforms the men rode under the blistering sun, drenched in sweat, stalked by disease and death, the water infrequent and often bad. Back from recruiting duty, Kearny followed the column, gathering up the sick.

Through July the Dodge expedition, now reduced to 200 men, trudged wearily west, nearing the Indians. On 14 July Colonel Dodge spotted a body of riders in the distance: Comanche warriors. For the first time in history, US Cavalry and Indians were to meet. Would the Indians prove friendly or hostile? A trooper was sent out to meet the Comanches; he extended his hand in a gesture of peace and the gesture was returned. Soon the Dragoons were escorted into the Comanche village for a friendly powwow – and some sights that few white men had ever seen. The troopers were treated to a show of Comanche horsemanship in which warriors

Above: *The capture of Washington by British Army and Navy forces during the War of 1812.*

Left: *Stephen Watts Kearny's cavalry career would coincide with American expansion until his death in 1848, soon after he helped secure a million square miles of territory to the United States in the Mexican War.*

Right: *General Winfield Scott led the successful attack on Fort George in the War of 1812. He was an American military hero until the early days of the Civil War.*

29

Opposite, top: *After the Revolutionary War, the cavalry saw little action for half a century.*

Opposite, far left: *Dress uniform for America's early mounted units.*

Opposite, near left: *American armies would retain their militia stamp into the nineteenth century.*

Above: *Colonel Johnson's engagement with Indians commanded by Tecumseh.*

Left: *A US Dragoon lieutenant of 1840.*

galloped about hanging from the sides of their mounts, and shooting arrows from under the horses' necks. Perhaps the Dragoons began at that point to understand the kind of fighters they would be up against. Leaving behind 39 more sick men, Dodge set out for the village of the Pawnee with only 183 more-or-less sound troopers.

The column pushed into the peaks and defiles of the Rockies, where grass and game declined as the terrain became more difficult. One afternoon Colonel Dodge was startled to see a group of his Indian scouts galloping toward him at full tilt, followed by a group of shouting Pawnee on horseback. There was a moment of raw fear before the scouts came close enough for their shouts of 'Hold fire!' to be heard. The Pawnee were simply providing a friendly welcome. Soon the troopers were touring the exotic environs of the Pawnee village, and Colonel Dodge was making his standard speech to the chiefs: 'We meet you as friends, not as enemies, to make peace with you, to shake hands with you. The great American Captain is at peace with all the white men in the world.' In return the chiefs handed over the abducted child, Matthew Martin, and received the Pawnee girl who had ridden with the expedition. As Dodge and the chiefs conferred, a group of Kiowa warriors rode whooping into the camp; they were presented with the girl of their village brought by the Dragoons. The meeting ended with warm assurances of eternal peace. On 25 July the column set out on the long road home, with the sick list growing every day; among others, painter Catlin was now critically ill (he eventually recovered).

Finally, on 15 August, the bedraggled and emaciated remnant of the Dodge expedition rode back into Fort Gibson. The last of the surviving sick arrived some days later. In a two-month expedition of over 500 miles, 90 Dragoons had died without a single hostile action. Of the rest, few were sound, some were permanently disabled. It seemed a most unpromising beginning for the US Cavalry's career of subduing the Indians of the West. Yet the expedition must be accounted a success. Soon the Kiowas and Osages were declaring peace, and the tribes later to be forcibly relocated to the West – the Creeks, Cherokee, some of the Seminoles, and others – proved susceptible to Dragoon shows of strength in a series of ensuing expeditions. In short, the Dodge expedition proved the usefulness of the horse soldier in the West: the cavalryman was there to stay.

The Dragoons then began to settle into the territory and the job, due largely to the tireless exertions of Stephen Watts Kearny, who was named colonel of the First Dragoons after the departure of Henry Dodge. Subsequent expeditions, such as one Kearny led for 800 miles in mid-1835, experienced little of the sickness of men and horses that had devastated the first Dodge expedition. Under Kearny, the Yellow-

legs were becoming canny and tough.

In 1836 Congress created the Second Dragoons to help suppress the Seminoles in Florida. This proved to be an inglorious and costly war of six years' duration, in which the whole apparatus of the US Army was unable to conquer a few hundred Seminole warriors. In those hellish swamps, the Second Dragoons were rarely mounted; what action they saw was mostly coping with small Indian raids – which was deadly enough work. By 1841 most of the Seminoles had gone off the warpath, and the war petered out. For a time the 2nd Dragoons were dismounted, but they were soon to return in anticipation of the Mexican War.

Meanwhile, Stephen Watts Kearny had continued to build and sharpen the First Dragoons in the West. In the long run it was perhaps he more than anyone else who established the quality and the tradition of the US Cavalry. His young cousin, Phil Kearny, was also to become a cavalryman of note; it was Phil Kearny who wrote the first US Cavalry manual in the late 1830s, based on a study of French techniques. In the decade before the Mexican War began in 1846, Stephen Watts Kearny's Dragoons fought no wars, but they were busy enough – keeping the Indians impressed from Louisiana to Michigan, adding three new forts to the chain of army

Left: *An 1857 sketch – highly idealized, in the style of the times – of a wagon train being attacked by hostile Indians.*

Above: *A blizzard on the plains visits hardship on the unfortunate men and animals caught in the teeth of the storm.*

Below: *The prototypical 'US Cavalry to the rescue' picture, titled 'Soldiers Coming' – Dodge's Re-enforcement.*

Main picture: *General Winfield Scott led the successful American attack on the Mexican fortress of Molino del Rey, en route to Mexico City.*

Left: *The Battle of Resaca de la Palma, Texas, 9 May 1846.*

Opposite: *Members of the Second Dragoons fight off an ambush by Mexican guerrillas in the Mexican War of 1846-8.*

moved that far, the British would get the idea. Guiding them was legendary mountain man Thomas Fitzpatrick, known to his Indian friends as 'Broken Hand.' Though they did bring along a few sheep and cattle, the Dragoons intended to live off the land, which they had come to know a great deal better than they had under Dodge in 1834. Soon they were riding alongside the great Oregon-bound wagon trains of the era. By 14 June they had arrived at Fort Laramie, not a fort but rather a frontier trading post run by the American Fur Company. It was a gathering place for thousands of Oregon-bound pioneers as well as Indians and assorted adventurers.

Kearny sent word to the local Sioux requesting a council meeting. Tribal leaders agreed, and on 16 June ceremoniously received the Dragoon officers – the first government troops they had ever dealt with. As the chiefs sat in a wide semi-circle on the plain, Kearny began, 'Sioux: I am glad to see you. Your Great Father has learned much of his red children and has sent me with a few braves to visit you. . . . I am opening a road for the white people, and your Great Father directs that his red children shall not attempt to close it.' He went on to warn the Sioux about the dangers of whiskey. When he was done the head chief rose and replied, 'If my people will be good to the whites, they will find that presents they are about to receive will come often. Father, this does very well and pleases me.' That was about all there was to it. For the Dragoons in the West, the business of Indian relations seemed to be going rather easily so far. The reason was probably that there were not yet enough settlers to worry the Indians in the region seriously. The Oregon settlers, after all, were only going through Sioux territory on their way across the mountains. Later, when they saw their lands being seized piece by piece, the Indians of the West would prove far less docile.

The expedition pushed on, reaching its goal by 30 June – the South Pass of the Rockies, 850 miles from their departure point of Fort Leavenworth. There, at the farthest point west that American soldiers had ever gathered, Kearny enjoyed a triumphant parade by his troops. Then the expedition headed for home, stopping on the way to parley with the Cheyenne and to put in an appearance at Bent's Fort on the New Mexico border – this to impress the Mexicans. On 1 August they were back in Fort Leavenworth. The Kearny expedition had traveled 2200 miles in 99 days and, in contrast to the Dodge expedition, had not lost a man. Thus the Dragoons had conquered their first enemy in the West, the land itself. Now they were ready for other battles, and those would come soon enough. In May 1846, Kearny received dispatches from Washington telling him that the United States was at war with Mexico.

The war had been in the offing for years. In 1845 President James K Polk took office with the stated goal of expansion and proceeded to do what he had been elected to do – secure New

posts along the Western frontier, keeping the Santa Fe Trail open, defending over a thousand miles of frontier. They did all that with about 600 men; the number of cavalrymen involved throughout their activities in the West was absurdly small compared to their importance.

In addition to his command of the First Dragoons, Kearny was put in charge of the Third Military Department in 1842, which made him responsible for much of the West. It was clear that his men were destined for more than continued skirmishes with the Indians. War with Mexico was becoming inevitable: the United States wanted Texas, New Mexico and California for its own. There was trouble brewing elsewhere too; as hundreds of settlers pushed north on the Oregon Trail, Britain became increasingly truculent about its claim to Oregon. In 1845 Kearny was ordered to make an expedition toward Oregon, to provide a show of strength for the benefit of the British as well as for the Indian tribes in the area. Kearny was ailing, as he had been since the rigors of the Dodge expedition (in fact he had only three years to live), but his expedition of 1845 was to be one of the legendary episodes in US Cavalry history.

On 19 May 1845, Stephen Watts Kearny and 250 men of the First Dragoons – Phil Kearny among them – rode out of Fort Leavenworth. Their goal was not Oregon as such but the South Pass of the Rockies, the trail to which lay across present Idaho and part of Wyoming. If they

Opposite, top: *Captain Charles May of the US Second Dragoons astonished the enemy at the Battle of Resaca de la Palma by charging Mexican artillery. He and his men gained the time needed for Zachary Taylor's infantry to advance and secure the victory.*

Above: *Charge of the Mexican Lancers at the Battle of Buena Vista.*

Right: *A cavalry recruitment poster for the Mexican War; traditionally, cavalry volunteers furnished their own horses and equipment. One inducement offered here is a 'mileage allowance' of 50 cents per day for use of the horse.*

Mexico and California by whatever means. The means turned out to be war, which Polk incited by sending troops into territory claimed by Mexico. (Texas, meanwhile, had voted itself into the Union.) The Mexican War was never to be a popular one, however; Americans wanted the land, but the means employed left a bad taste in their mouths.

Kearny received a second order from Washington, instructing him to recruit a thousand volunteers from Missouri and a force of Mormons. This was soon done and Kearny was ready to march on Santa Fe. By that time the Second Dragoons were already in the thick of it in Mexico.

General Zachary Taylor – later to be president – was fighting there with his euphemistically named 'Army of Observation'; with him were seven troops of the Second Dragoons. On 8 May Taylor used his infantry and artillery to rout the forces of General Manuel Arista in the Battle of Palo Alto. But General Arista was by no means finished after that day. As the Mexican general moved south with his army, Taylor and his forces followed, catching up with the enemy on the afternoon of 9 May, at Resaca de la Palma. There they found Arista well protected by his artillery, which was positioned to sweep the road on which the Americans were advancing.

Taylor opened up with his own artillery and got his infantry some way forward, but they came to a halt in the face of the Mexican cannon firing from across the shallow ravine of the Resaca. In desperation, Taylor did something that, had he been a West Point man, he would have learned never to do: he called up Dragoon Captain Charles May and told him, 'Charge, Captain! Charge, *nolens volens.*' (It is old military doctrine that cavalry must never charge artillery.) May trotted back to his men, who were waiting in columns of four with their heavy Prussian sabers drawn, and shouted, 'Remember your regiment and follow your officers!' With a snap of his arm he took the Dragoons

forward toward the Mexican artillery.

In short order the troopers were galloping wildly into a storm of canister from the enemy guns; soon a number of saddles were empty. Captain May and a few Dragoons made it over the Mexican breastworks and exercised their sabers. The rest, their horses balking before the breastworks, rode across the enemy line and around to the rear, driving the Mexicans away from their guns. Then they had to force their way back through the enemy artillery position to regain the American lines. The Mexicans quickly reoccupied their cannons, but the charge had given Taylor's infantry time to advance. Arista's Mexicans were routed, the Dragoons hastening them on their way.

All in all, it was a good thing that Zachary Taylor didn't fight by the book at Resaca de la Palma. The gallant charge of the Dragoons had won the day. Soon the Second Dragoons had a new coat of arms, depicting a saber-wielding horseman charging a Mexican cannoneer. In the battle General Arista had nearly 800 casualties; American losses were 39 killed and fewer than 100 wounded.

A month later the First Dragoons were marching down the Santa Fe Trail under Stephen Watts Kearny, moving against Mexican forces in New Mexico. Kearny was soon to be appointed a brevet brigadier general. He and his motley group of Dragoons, Missouri Mounted Volunteers, infantry, artillery, Indian scouts and assorted others – some 1700 in all, with 16 field guns – were ordered to conquer New Mexico. Challenging Kearny's men in the territory was the army of Mexican Governor Manuel Armijo. Kearny drove his column relentlessly, halving rations to save time, sometimes making over 30 miles a day. By early August the rigors of the march were taking their toll; graves began ap-

pearing in the wake of the column. By the time they approached Las Vegas the men had marched nearly 1000 miles; at that point the news came that Governor Armijo was waiting for them before Santa Fe with 10,000 men. Undaunted, Kearny hurried on to Las Vegas, ready to fight. Contrary to reports, however, there proved to be no Mexican resistance in the city: Kearny marched in unopposed and raised the flag. Gearing up for action, the column moved on toward the expected battle at Santa Fe. But at the approach of the Americans, Governor Armijo bolted. In reality, he had commanded few troops – most of the Mexican Army was fighting on its own soil in the south. On 18 August Kearny and his column rode peacefully into Santa Fe, raised the flag over the Palace of Governors and declared New Mexico a United States possession. He had conquered a huge territory without firing a shot. Now it was time to move on to the next objective, which would not prove so easy – California.

On 25 September 1846, Kearny and his men set out on the 1000-mile march to California. His five companies of Dragoons were dressed in blue flannel uniforms, each carrying two pistols, a single-shot carbine and a Bowie knife. They had left their sabers at Fort Leavenworth; though Dragoons were still counted in sabers, the age-old weapon of the horse soldier (as opposed to numbers of men), commanders were beginning to realize the limits of the saber's usefulness. Miles behind Kearny rode the newly formed Mormon Battalion, led by Captain Philip

St George Cooke, with orders to follow Kearny and build a wagon road. This time the bulk of Kearny's heterogeneous detachment walked; most of the horses and mules that had died or given out on the way to Santa Fe had not been replaced. All the Dragoons rode mules, many of them already broken down. It was an ominous commencement to a long and frustrating campaign.

However, the first signs were hopeful. On 6 October the column was greeted by mountain man Kit Carson, who brought good news from California: irregulars and US Navy men had taken the territory for the United States and installed as governor the famous explorer John C Frémont, who had become an Army Major. Kearny thought things over, then sent three companies of Dragoons back to Santa Fe. The remaining two companies he placed on the best mounts he had and ordered Carson, who was serving as a temporary lieutenant, to lead the column to California.

The route lay across a fearsome obstacle course of gorges and desert. Of all the difficult marches in US Cavalry history, this one was to prove among the worst. The diary of a participant describes its early stages: 'The only consolation a man has is that his mule is feeding and may be able to carry him another day farther on the journey – our pack animals are getting in a most pitiable condition – their backs are cut all to pieces – and so poor and weak that they can hardly be goaded along.' Water was plentiful enough, as they marched along the Rio Grande

on, sometimes literally pushing their mounts ahead of them and eating mostly horsemeat, bad news arrived from California: Mexican Californians had revolted against US rule, conquered all of California south of San Luis Obispo and installed a Mexican governor in place of Frémont. On 3 December they were at Warner's Ranch, 60 miles from San Diego, nearly 1900 miles from Fort Leavenworth. There they learned the full extent of the counterrevolution – Mexicans controlled the entire state except for San Francisco, San Diego and Monterey.

Kearny requested supplies from American Commodore Stockton in San Diego: none were forthcoming. The Dragoons had managed to secure some remounts intended for the Mexicans, and a few volunteers, Marines and sailors joined the column. Learning on 5 December that a Mexican Army led by General Andres Pico lay nine miles distant, Kearny moved his weary column forward. The very idea of mounting an offensive with his played-out men and mounts was something of an absurdity, but that was what Kearny determined to try. It was what he had marched here for, after all.

In the early morning of 6 December, in a freezing drizzle, Kearny moved to the attack. The Mexicans, having been alerted, were waiting for him in front of the village of San Pasqual, which lay in a narrow valley. All the Americans could do was sweep in one end and hope to drive the enemy out the other. Fifty Dragoons charged into the Mexicans at a gallop; after emptying several American saddles and shooting Kit Carson's horse from under him, the Mexicans scattered back around the valley. For a few moments things seemed to be going well. Then the Americans, smelling victory, made a disorderly advance on into the valley. Their impetuousity invited disaster, and disaster struck on cue. Suddenly the Dragoons found themselves flanked by Mexican lancers, who closed in

Opposite, top: The dressy Dragoon uniform of 1851 had come a long way from the slapdash garb of the Revolutionary War. From left: Colonel, Sergeant Major, Musician.

Above: Kentucky cavalrymen played a distinguished part in the victory of Buena Vista, Mexico, although Scott's infantry forces were far more numerous.

Right: Colonel William S Harney commanded the Second Dragoons at this fight near Medelia, not far from Vera Cruz. Later he served under Philip Kearny at Churubusco, in the final push toward Mexico City.

and then along the Gila River, but food was a continuing problem; their cattle were dying on the trail, local Indians were sometimes willing to sell them food, sometimes not.

In the last week of November, Kearny and his starving, half-naked and exhausted men – and a few animals in similar straits – crossed the Colorado into California. The territory in front of them was, if anything, worse than what they had already crossed – there was little but heat and assorted shades of sand. As the men staggered

and broke apart Kearny's attack in brief and bloody fighting. Americans were lanced and lassoed off their horses to be dispatched on the ground; Kearny was wounded while fencing with an enemy. The American attack repulsed, the Mexican lancers rode away from San Pasqual leaving 19 Americans dead and 15 wounded. Minus mounts and supplies, Kearny and his men limped to the San Bernardo Ranch. San Pasqual had been a most ill-advised and - executed attack, with predictably dismal results. Though only a small skirmish by most wartime standards, it was the bloodiest day of the war in California and a humiliating defeat for the Dragoons.

Kearny's men held on in their camp for days while Pico's forces pressed in on them. Finally, on 11 December, reinforcements arrived from Commodore Stockton. Pico then pulled away, and the Americans trudged on to the Pacific Coast at San Diego, the endpoint of one of the most grueling marches in the nation's history. Perhaps they found some satisfaction in that. They certainly found some in January 1847, when Kearny, recovered from his wound, led combined American forces to defeat the Mexicans at Los Angeles. Once again, and for good, the American flag flew above the city.

This victory was soon followed by General Winfield Scott's successes in Mexico at Buena Vista, Vera Cruz and elsewhere; these were largely infantry affairs. But Scott had noticed the fighting spirit of cavalryman Phil Kearny, Stephen Watts Kearny's young nephew. Phil had raised a crack outfit of his own, the Gray Horse Troop, which became Scott's guard of honor. In August of 1847, Scott was pursuing his campaign against General Santa Anna. The Second Dragoons were commanded by Colonel William S Harney and included the men of Phil Kearny's troop. On 20 August the opposing armies were poised for battle at Churubusco, near Mexico City. Phil Kearny asked Scott for a transfer from headquarters duty to the battle line, and Scott complied.

The armies of Generals Scott and Santa Anna crashed together and the fighting surged back and forth, American infantry and Dragoons pushing into the Mexicans' center and routing them. Kearny and the other horsemen pursued the fleeing enemy infantry with their sabers. When a few Dragoons had gotten ahead of the infantry, Kearny rode forward, pistol in one hand, saber in the other, the reins in his teeth. The Dragoons had advanced so far that Scott ordered a bugler to sound the recall. Kearny later admitted he heard the recall, but added, 'I was sure it was not for me.' He kept advancing, with some dozen Dragoons, until they found themselves dismounted right in front of the Mexican lines. As the Mexicans swarmed around them, the Dragoons formed a circle and fought with sabers; as a man was killed, the one behind used his body for a shield. Finally, a few of them tore away. Phil Kearny leaped on his horse and

Insert top left: *An aging General Winfield Scott (nicknamed by his men 'Old Fuss and Feathers') sat for this portrait after the Mexican War.*

Main picture: *The Battle of Vera Cruz, showing the American squadron bombarding the Mexican fortress.*

Above: *Scott's triumphal entry into the Mexican capital in 1847 presaged the acquisition of vast new Western territories, which a comparative handful of US Cavalrymen would have to safeguard and pacify.*

Charles Schreyvogel painted this scene wherein a cavalryman covered by two comrades rescues his bunkmate from attacking Indians.

somehow escaped, but not before enemy grape-shot claimed his left arm. It did not damage his military career, which would continue into the Civil War – Kearny was used to riding with the reins in his teeth.

The Americans won the day at Churubusco, and on 13 September 1847, Winfield Scott led his victorious forces into Mexico City. The Mexicans soon asked for peace. By hook and by crook, President Polk had made good on his vow to secure Texas, New Mexico and California, adding a million square miles to US territory. Though horse soldiers had been in action throughout the war, neither Winfield Scott nor Zachary Taylor had used them in anything approaching their true capacity. American generals simply had not yet discovered the real potential of mounted units. Robert E Lee and Jeb Stuart would teach them that lesson.

After the war with Mexico, Stephen Watts Kearny had only a year to live; most of that year was spent in a bitter wrangle with fractious John C Frémont, who was court-martialed for defying Kearny's orders in California. But Kearny died with a solid accomplishment behind him: more than anyone else, he had built the cavalry into a proud, effective and firmly established branch of the US Army.

In 1849 gold was discovered in California, and the stream of settlers heading west swelled to a flood that would scarcely ever abate. The Dragoons and the army turned their attention to policing the trails and settlements of California, Utah and Oregon. There were continual calls from settlers to suppress – often to annihilate – the Indians. The army had to walk a narrow course between the professedly benevolent attitude of the government toward nominally peaceful Indians and the fearful and hostile attitude of the settlers toward any and all Indians, whose lands the settlers wanted and were getting, piece by piece. It was an impossible situation, a kettle boiling toward eventual violence and tragedy, just as other tensions were simmering toward eruption of the Civil War.

If Stephen Watts Kearny shepherded the Dragoons in their infancy and adolescence, it was his old partner Philip St George Cooke who seasoned them into maturity after Kearny's death. Cooke had been a Dragoon since the Dodge expedition, growing up along with the regiment. After the Mexican War he was named Lieutenant Colonel of the Second Dragoons; in the absence of his superior, Colonel Harney, he was its real commander. Thus Cooke took over the reins of Indian fighting in the West. Though there was never to be an all-out Indian offensive before the Civil War, army statistics of the 1850s record 22 'wars' and 37 'engagements' that saw casualties. It was a nerve-wracking, ever-widening guerrilla warfare that Cooke and his men waged.

In 1855 President Franklin Pierce's secretary of war, Jefferson Davis – who would become president of the Confederacy five years later – decreed four new army regiments, which raised the number of men in arms from 10,000 to 15,000. Two of the new regiments were mounted, but this time they were called not Dragoons but the First and Second Cavalry – the first units so named in the US Army. The reasons for the new designation are hazy: it is quite possible that it had to do with the autocratic Davis, who kept the new outfits separate in command so as to put his favorites at their helms. Among the officers of the cavalry were a number of men destined to be much heard of in the Civil War, most of them on the Confederate side. Commanding the First Cavalry was Edwin V Sumner, later a Union general; his lieutenant colonel was to be one of the great Southern generals, Joseph E Johnston. Officers of the Second Cavalry included such future Confederates as Albert Sidney Johnston, William J Hardee, John B Hood and Lieutenant Colonel Robert E Lee.

The only real differences between the old Dragoons and the new Cavalry were in name and dress; both were essentially light cavalry, as were the divisions called Mounted Rifles. In theory, each kind of outfit carried different weapons; in practice, they carried whatever was handy: old breechloading smoothbore Hall carbines, cavalry musketoons and a few of the new breechloading Sharps carbines. Some troopers also sported Colt six-shooters, replacing the old single-shot horse pistols. Usually left at home was the saber, which was manifestly of little use in fighting Indians. As was often the case, it was the enlisted men who knew better than their officers what worked on the battlefield

Above: *Schreyvogel's dramatic painting* Fight for the Water Hole *gives a sense of the unequal struggle between white man and Indian for possession of the West.*

Left: *Frederic Remington's colorful and authentic portraits of Western Americana include this view of off-duty US Cavalrymen playing cards* – Dispute Over a Deal.

and what didn't; to the end of his career Cooke favored carrying sabers, and army brass refused to consider the repeating carbine until well into the Civil War. It was an era of bewilderingly rapid developments in weaponry, so the inertia of tradition was probably inevitable.

By the 1850s the cavalrymen had fallen into habits of dress as random and makeshift as their weaponry. Their clothes were a heterogeneous collection of official issue of various periods supplemented *ad hoc* by each trooper. A young cavalryman of the 1850s wrote home from the frontier, 'I wish you could see me in my scouting costume. Mounted on my mule [with] corduroy pants; a hickory or blue flannel shirt, cut down in front, studded with pickets and worn outside; a slouched hat and long beard, cavalry boots worn over the pants, knife and revolver belted to the side and a double barrel gun across the pommel, complete the costume, as truly serviceable as it is unmilitary.' After 1847 army horsemen changed from a saddle much like the

modern English to the Grimsley saddle, which was standard until the coming of the McClellan saddle just before the Civil War.

In the West the army tended to use infantry to hold posts, mounted men actually to engage the Indians. In that era such campaigns always proved fairly short and more or less successful, however bloody. There were two non-Indian campaigns of interest just before the war. In 1856 Kansas was about to become a state and was torn by factions for and against its coming in with slaves. Abolitionists were moving their sympathizers into the area and pro-slavery men were raiding from Missouri. It was a volatile situation, emblematic of the pressure that was building all over the country. Jefferson Davis sent Cooke into Kansas to keep the peace and the Dragoons did so – just barely – with an even-handedness that won respect from both factions. Meanwhile, Colonel Sumner and the First Cavalry separated gangs led by fanatic abolitionist John Brown and a Missouri pro-slave hood-

Above: *A realistic interpretation of the Western emigration experience: a view of Devil's Gate Landmark on the Oregon Trail through Central Wyoming.*

Right: *This romanticized pastoral scene, titled* Bedding Down for the Night, *was painted by Benjamin Franklin Reinhart. Few pioneers would have recognized themselves (or their livestock) in this tableau.*

Left: *Painter George Catlin accompanied the Dodge Expedition and suffered many hardships, including a near-fatal illness, in his quest to capture the receding frontier on canvas. This impressive oil of Chief Keokuk, who sought peace with encroaching settlers on behalf of the Saux and Fox tribes, was painted in 1835.*

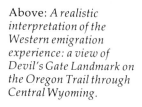

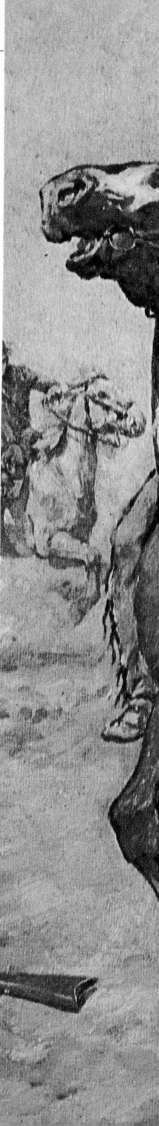

Above: *US Cavalrymen defend their stockade against marauding Indians, in this Schreyvogel painting that epitomizes the mythos of the American West.*

Left: *Many cavalrymen who served on the frontier would bring their hard-won experience into the Civil War, where American Cavalry came into its own. Their uniforms might be either blue or grey, but the saber remained a badge of distinction.*

Right: *Schreyvogel's* The Duel *pits a skilled Plains warrior against a saber-wielding trooper. There was perhaps only one thing for which the native American was truly grateful to the white man – the horse, introduced by the Spanish into the New World.*

Right: *Cavalryman Albert Sidney Johnston commanded the army of the Republic of Texas before he served in the Mexican War. His promising Confederate Army career would be cut short by a mortal wound at Shiloh in 1862.*

Above: *Bactrian camels were imported and tried out as cavalry mounts in the Western desert before the Civil War, but this costly experiment was short-lived.*

Right: *The diverse uniforms of the newly formed Confederate Army in 1861.*

lum; if the two gangs had started shooting, the Civil War might have started then and there. With the Dragoons maintaining the peace, Kansas had calmed down by autumn of 1856, and most of the horse soldiers returned to post-duty and Indian-fighting at Forts Leavenworth and Riley.

The next year saw one of the odder episodes in US Cavalry history. President James Buchanan determined to reassert government sovereignty over the Mormons, who had long had a rocky and ambiguous relationship with Washington, in the Territory of Utah. To Mormons, all others were 'gentiles' without jurisdiction over the Saints. Buchanan sent a detachment of the Second Cavalry under Colonel Albert Sidney Johnston toward Salt Lake City to uphold Federally appointed authorities in Utah. Advised of their coming, Mormon leader Brigham Young vowed defiance: 'Woe, woe to that man who comes here to unlawfully interfere with my affairs. Woe, woe to those men who come here to unlawfully meddle with me and this people.' While the Federal expedition trudged through the Rockies during the winter, Young began to organize an army.

For the horse soldiers it was an awful winter. Cooke and the Dragoons pushed through the mountains trying to catch up with Johnston's infantry detachment. Temperatures fell to 44 degrees below zero Fahrenheit, with vicious winds, blizzards and deep snow. Only ten of nearly 150 Dragoon horses survived the trek. The two detachments finally pulled into Fort Bridger on the road to Salt Lake City, where they rested in a morass of trooper disaffection and command wrangles between Cooke and Johnston. At length they learned that something of a

political settlement had been patched up between the US Governor of Utah and Brigham Young, which let the air out of the conflict and saved face for everyone. However, General Johnston insisted on parading his forces into Salt Lake City. That parade, on 26 June 1857, was a singular spectacle. In order not to countenance this show of US authority, the Mormons had pulled out of the city lock, stock and barrel, leaving nothing but empty buildings to witness Johnston's display. When the cavalry left, the Mormons moved right back in.

Now the Dragoons and Cavalry went back to Indian management for some time. In 1858 there was a short-lived attempt to mount Dragoons on camels; it proved an imaginative but useless experiment. Then, in 1860, the long-simmering tensions between North and South erupted, and the horse soldiers were caught up in the resulting explosion to find their greatest challenge, one that divided them as it divided the nation.

UNIFORMS OF REGULAR CONFEDERATE TROOPS.

Infantry.   Cavalry.   Artillery.   Louisiana Zouaves.   Washington Artillery of New Orleans.   Mississippi Rifles.   Henry Infantry of Georgia.   Alabama Light Infantry.   Marine Battery, Montgomery Cavalry.

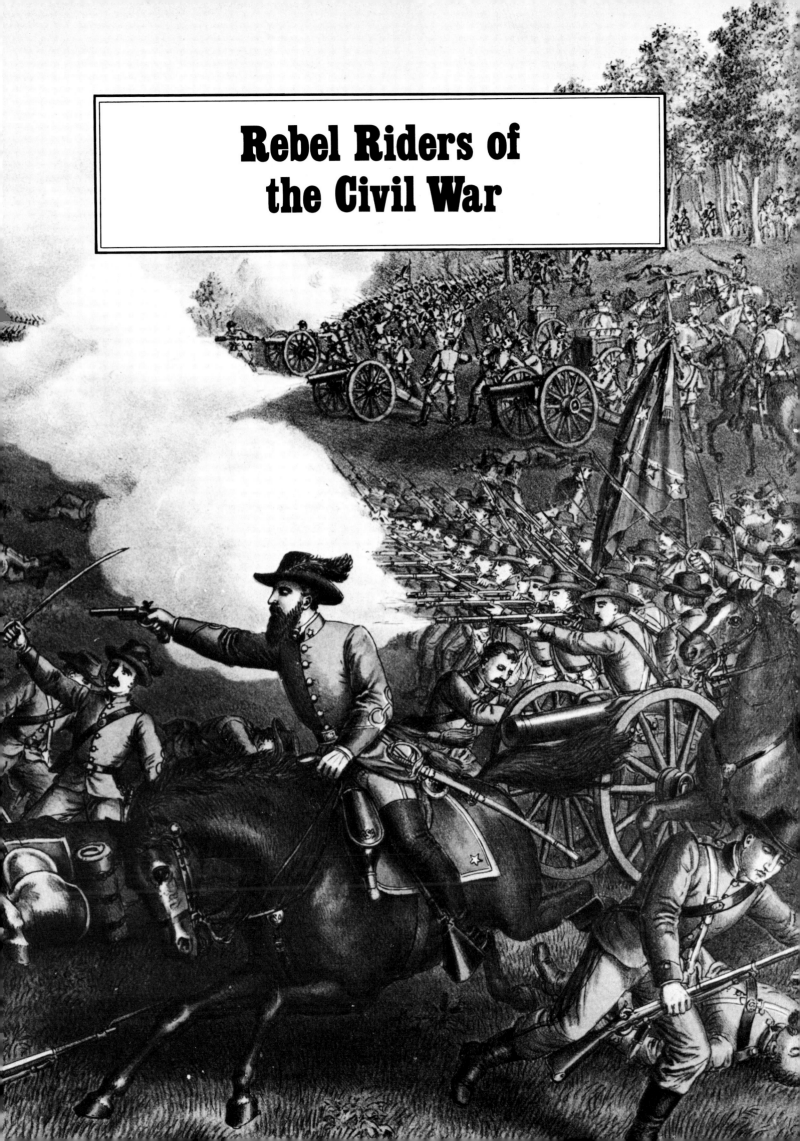

Rebel Riders of the Civil War

In 1861 the complex dynamic of tensions that had long simmered beneath the surface of American life, most of them centered on the bitter question of black slavery, erupted into the Civil War. States, towns, friends, families split into their chosen loyalties – and so did members of the US Army. Former Dragoon commander and secretary of war Jefferson Davis became president of the Confederate States of America. His military officers included other former Dragoons and Cavalrymen like Robert E Lee, Joseph E Johnston and a handsome young man of 28 named James Ewell Brown Stuart, known to

most as 'Jeb,' and to his West Point classmates as 'Beauty.' The story of cavalry in the Civil War can begin with Jeb Stuart and the riders of the Confederacy, because in the first part of the war it was the Rebel riders who created and pursued the art of warfare on horseback with a dash and brilliance it had rarely had in modern history and would never have again – except for the later exploits of the Union Cavalry, after they had absorbed the hard-won lessons taught them by the Confederate horsemen.

When the war began, cavalry had never had a clear and vital function in the US Army: even after 25 years, it remained a minor branch of the service. But Jefferson Davis and his generals understood well the true potential of the mounted arm. Moreover, most Southern cavalrymen, unlike their Yankee counterparts, had come from a rural and agricultural background and were therefore used to riding and to shooting. And the Confederacy could draw on the superb stock of horses from Virginia, Kentucky and North Carolina.

In the initial engagements of the war, the North was bested in most respects, not least in the area of cavalry employment. On 21 July 1861 came the initial great battle, the First Bull Run, known in the South as First Manassas. (The South tended to name both armies and battles after towns, the North after the nearest stream). On that day Northern forces under General Irvin McDowell were routed by the forces of General P G T Beauregard. It was in this battle that a Southern general and former mathematics professor named Thomas J Jackson led his men to a stout defense that earned him (and his division) the name 'Stonewall.' And it was also then that Jeb Stuart first showed his mettle in handling

Previous pages: An idealized portrayal of Confederate and Union Cavalry leaders clashing on the field of battle.

Right: James Ewell Brown (Jeb) Stuart, the daring and successful Confederate cavalry leader who became a legend in his own time.

Below: Jeb Stuart's cavalrymen returning from a raid.

cavalry, screening the Confederate forces and driving from the field a force of grandly clad New York Zouaves. As for the Federal Cavalry at Bull Run – it appears that many of the horses bolted and their riders were more than happy to go along.

After the battle Stuart and his men screened the Confederate forces. A distinguished visitor, Prince Napoleon of France, observed of Stuart and his men: 'Nothing is as picturesque as the Southern cavalry. They wear the most impossible outfits: mostly rags, hats without bottoms, boots without soles. Yet they could make Don Bazan jealous of their martial bearing and countenance.' Of Stuart himself, the Prince noted, 'He had something of Murat's weakness for the vanities of military parade. He betrayed this latter quality in his jaunty uniform, which consisted of a small gray jacket, trousers of the same stuff, and over them high military boots, a yellow silk sash, and a gray slouch hat surmounted by a sweeping black plume.' Finally, the prince admired Stuart's 'Jovian beard,' which in fact was intended to hide a weak chin.

Indeed, Jeb Stuart was the archetypal stuff of legend and romance, something out of a not-very-good Hollywood epic. He had come up in the normal military fashion, graduating from West Point and serving with the cavalry in the West. Along with a number of US Army officers, many of whom were Southern, Stuart resigned from the Army in 1861 to take a commission as a lieutenant colonel in the Confederate Army. After First Bull Run he was made a brigadier general, and a year later, major general, with command of all Robert E Lee's cavalry.

What was uncommon about Jeb Stuart was his extravagance in dress and manner – he wrote and recited his own poetry, mostly concerning his exploits, and when he rode into action he was accompanied by a black banjo player named Sweeny. The same extravagance was reflected in his fighting style. During the course of the war he developed the revolutionary tactics of the strategic raid – striking behind enemy lines at Northern communications, supply bases, factories and railroads. This kind of work required speed, daring, stealth and unflinching courage – which were exactly the prime personality traits of Jeb Stuart. He reminds one of the ancient horse warriors, and of an eighteenth-century general's observation that 'The cavalryman who is not dead before 35 is a scoundrel.' Jeb Stuart was not destined to be any such scoundrel. His fearless and flamboyant style soon won him still another nickname: 'The Cavalier.'

Right: *Union and Confederate troopers duel during the Battle of Fair Oaks (Seven Pines), 31 May 1862.*

In the summer of 1862, Union General George B McClellan led his new and immense Army of the Potomac into Virginia in an 'On to Richmond' campaign. At that time Stuart's cavalry were under General Joseph E Johnston, who was opposing the Union campaign up the peninsula between Virginia's York and James Rivers. Stuart already excelled at scouting, screening, and harassment of Union supply lines – tactics not unlike those of Robert E Lee's father, Light-Horse Harry, in the Revolution. As intended, the Southern horse kept McClellan in the dark as to Rebel movements and numbers; for the South the great advantage of this was that McClellan consistently believed he was outnumbered two to one, when the reverse was more nearly the case. An escalating series of engagements ensued, and at the end of May, close to Richmond, Confederate General Johnston was wounded. His replacement was General Robert E Lee. In his first days of command, Lee renamed his force the Army of Northern Virginia and sent Stuart and 1200 of his riders on a raiding and scouting mission that was to become the first major element of the Stuart legend: a ride clean around McClellan's Army of the Potomac.

Previous pages:
Confederate cavalry cross the Potomac (11 June 1863) in the ill-starred invasion of Maryland and Pennsylvania.

Right: *Major-General Fitzhugh (Fitz) Lee, nephew of Robert E Lee.*

Riding with Stuart were Lee's son and nephew, Colonels W H F (Rooney) and Fitzhugh (Fitz) Lee respectively. They set out on 12 June, singing 'Kathleen Mavourneen,' Stuart's favorite tune, accompanied by his banjo player. Their primary goal was to scout out the arrangements of McClellan's right wing, the corps of General Fitz-John Porter. Soon the Rebels made contact with the Union 56th Cavalry, which made a stand at Topotomoy Creek. Though outnumbered six to one, Stuart's men charged and routed the Yankees. Word went back to the Union Cavalry commander in that area, none other than Philip St George Cooke, who by then was the father-in-law of Jeb Stuart. Cooke sent out a detachment intended to kill or capture his daughter's husband.

By then Stuart had scouted Porter's corps and found it vulnerable, unsupported by McClellan – 'in the air,' as it was called. Knowing Cooke would be on his trail, Stuart decided his best bet was to continue on around the Army of the Potomac, cutting across Union communications and raiding as he went, which meant burning and destroying anything to do with the US Army. Slowed by an infantry detachment, Cooke's men pursued ineffectively. When they finally reached the Chickahominy River, east of the Federal lines, the Rebels found themselves in a spot – the Federals were closing in behind and the river was flooded. A few days later one of his officers was to quiz Stuart, 'That was a tight place at the river, General. If the enemy had come down on us, you would have been compelled to surrender.' The reply was pure Stuart: 'No, one other course was left – to die game.'

In fact, what Stuart did on the banks of the Chickahominy was eminently practical: he had his men tear apart a barn and rebuild a burnt bridge. The Rebel Cavalry got over that bridge,

Below: *Union General Fitz-John Porter, who was blamed by his superiors for the Confederate success at Second Bull Run. He spent 23 years trying to clear his name, and ultimately succeeded.*

torching it behind them just as Cooke's men arrived and started shooting. The Rebel riders reached Richmond on 15 June; they had ridden around the enemy, 100 miles in four days, fighting much of the way, and had lost a total of only four men captured. With the information Stuart gave him about Porter's vulnerability, Lee ordered an all-out attack. Back behind Union lines, Stuart's victim Philip St George Cooke was soon taken off active duty; the old Dragoon was scarcely to fight again, though he stayed in the army until 1873.

Stonewall Jackson's corps fell on Porter on 26 June while Lee hit McClellan's front. But Jackson was unwontedly slow and indecisive; on that day and subsequent encounters of what came to be known as the Seven Days' Battles, Lee was unable to seriously damage Union forces, due mostly to the inexplicable lassitude of Jackson. Nonetheless, the always-overcautious McClellan, still convinced his army was greatly outnumbered, pulled away from Richmond to the south. Stuart raided around the Federals, gathering in Yankee guns and supplies, even attacking a Federal gunboat on the Pamunkey River and chasing it downstream. Reportedly, Stuart was laughing so hard during this escapade that he could hardly stay on his horse – it was like mosquitoes chasing a whale.

The Cavalier and his men returned to their duties of screening Lee's forces, keeping Federal Cavalry at a safe distance. Finally McClellan sailed away with his army; Lee had failed to conquer the Yankees, but he had persuaded them that Virginia was not an especially safe place to bivouac. Typically, Stuart wrote a flowery poem called 'The Ride Around McClellan,' which he was willing to recite to the young ladies of Richmond with very little encouragement.

Northern hopes for victory now shifted to the Federal Army of Virginia under blustering General John Pope, whom President Lincoln ordered to strike Lee. Pope began his campaign effectively enough, sending two brigades of cavalry 20 miles ahead to scout. Among the officers of this detachment was General John Buford, of whom much will be heard later. Buford had the then-radical notion that cavalry would be better off leaving their sabers at home and fighting like dragoons, that is, dismounted. Pope's cavalry did their job for a while but, as usual for Federal Cavalry in those days, the units were too small and scattered for decisive action. Still, during their ride some of these Federals dismounted with their carbines and did a good job of delaying Stuart's cavalry, who were in the vanguard of Lee's infantry. Moreover, a Union raid on Stuart's camp captured a handsome prize indeed: the Cavalier's plumed hat.

On 22 August Lee ordered Stuart to ride behind Pope and cut his rail line. Stuart rode out declaring, 'I intend to make the Yankees pay dearly for that hat.' In the ensuing raid the Southern horsemen not only hit the railroad, destroying Catlett's Station, but raided Pope's camp as well. Pope was away, and it was raining buckets. Ensconced inside a tent, a Federal officer had just proposed a toast: 'This is something like comfort,' he said, raising his glass; 'I hope Jeb Stuart won't disturb us tonight.' At that moment 2000 Rebel cavalry descended whooping onto the camp. The Yankee officer dropped his toddy, screaming 'There he is, by God!' In the confused action that ensued, some of the Federals found themselves trapped in their fallen tents and sabered from the outside. The Cavalier's men rode away with most of the Yankee stores, including Pope's dress coat. Stuart had gotten his revenge, and later had the additional pleasure of receiving a note from Pope asking to exchange their captured accoutrements.

Then Lee moved out to deal with General Pope. Stuart and his men screened the Confederate movement, skirmishing constantly, and rode ahead of Stonewall Jackson to a position on Pope's flank. In the process, Stuart's men tore up Federal railroads and pounced on a Federal supply dump at Manassas Junction. The ragged and hungry Confederates, cavalry and infantry, were most delighted with the latter; an observer wrote, 'To see a starving man eating lobster salad and drinking Rhine wine, barefooted and in tatters, was curious; the whole thing incredible.'

Pope remained blind as Lee and Jackson closed around him. In the ensuing Second Battle of Bull Run, on 29-30 August, Union forces were routed in yet another humiliating defeat, losing 13,000 casualties and vast quantities of supplies; Southern losses were some 10,000. Pope's retreat was covered by cavalry under old Dragoon Phil Kearny, one-armed but hard-fighting as ever. On 1 September, though, Kearny was shot dead off his horse as he charged the advancing enemy: with his death the North lost the nearest thing they ever had to a Yankee Jeb Stuart.

Opposite: General George B McClellan, the dilatory Union leader whom President Lincoln finally replaced as commander of the Army of the Potomac.

Below: General McClellan takes leave of the Army of the Potomac, accompanied by his successor, Ambrose Burnside (A R Waud drawing).

After the Second Bull Run (or, as the South has it, Second Manassas) Robert E Lee knew that he could depend absolutely on Jeb Stuart and his men to be both the eyes of his army and a gallant fighting force in their own right. Thus was formed a triumvirate that would spell victory for another year: Lee, Jackson and Stuart. Finally, cavalry had found its place on the American battlefield.

Lee and his Army of Northern Virginia had whipped McClellan and Pope. Now, Lee reasoned, was the time to invade the North and get the war over with. It was his first mistake, and it was to prove a big one.

Lee's immediate goals were to shake up and demoralize the North, to cut the railroads, secure food and supplies, and to stir up and perhaps even enlist Confederate sympathizers in Maryland. To those ends the Army of Northern Virginia crossed the Potomac into Maryland on 4 September 1862. Next day Jeb Stuart took his cavalry over, guarding Lee's rear. On the way

north Stuart stopped off in Urbana to plan strategy and, not least, to flirt with the local girls. A ball was gotten up, but while the Confederate officers danced and flirted, Yankee Cavalry appeared in town. Making apologies, Stuart and his officers rode off, chased the Yankees away and returned to dance some more.

Lee continued north, dispatching Stuart to help Jackson take Harper's Ferry, where a few years earlier Lee himself had led the US Army detachment that captured abolitionist John Brown. But Lee was pursued by the gremlins that seemed to afflict his operations every time he left Southern soil: an order with full descriptions of his dispositions was found in a field by a Union soldier. The order was incongruously wrapped around two cigars. The .plans were soon in the hands of General McClellan, who put his Army of the Potomac on the move to crush General Lee.

But McClellan moved a little too slowly. Lee learned from Stuart about the orders on the same night they were lost. At that point his forces were dangerously scattered in operations all over the area. Nonetheless, Lee decided to stand and fight on the banks of Antietam Creek. His decision had to do with his accurate knowledge of all McClellan's movements, of which Stuart's men kept him abreast, and with his low estimate of McClellan as a fighting general. As usual, Lee was entirely correct in judging his opponent.

On 14 August the Battle of Antietam (the Confederacy called it Sharpsburg) was joined. In a day of confused fighting, the bloodiest single day of the war, the Confederates held their line by a thread, thanks both to the brilliance of Lee and his generals and to the confusion of McClel-lan's command. Despite the appalling casualties – 12,410 for the North and 13,724 for the South – the result was in fact a stalemate, but in the long run it significantly benefitted the Union. Simply because it was not another disaster, the North was content to call Antietam a victory. In its wake, Abraham Lincoln issued the Emancipation Proclamation, which turned the war once and for all into a moral crusade against slavery. Though the Proclamation only declared Southern slaves to be freed, and thus in reality freed none at all, it was morally unthinkable after that point for any European country to intervene for the South – which had previously been a real possibility. A second result of Antietam was that Lee pulled back to Virginia, not exactly defeated, but by no means victorious.

As the two armies maneuvered, the Cavalier and his men kept Lee abreast of Federal activities, but did not neglect to reconnoiter some parties and balls, where Stuart recited original poems and anagrams. Finally, Lee ordered the Southern Cavalry to raid north as far as Pennsylvania, riding around McClellan again to scout and to steal horses. The cavalry left on what would be immortalized as the Chambersburg Raid. Riding with Stuart were 1800 men and officers, including Wade Hampton (grandson of the Revolutionary cavalryman of the same name), Rooney Lee, and William 'Grumble' Jones. Also along were horse artillery under 22-year-old John Pelham, the most brilliant cannoneer of the Confederacy, soon to be dubbed 'the gallant Pelham' for his actions during the battle of Fredericksburg. At daylight on 9 October, the Confederate riders crossed the Potomac into Maryland.

Above: *The Union victory at Antietam, Maryland, 17 September 1862.*

Left: Harper's Weekly *published this sketch of Confederate Cavalry crossing the Potomac to invade Maryland.*

Right: *Confederate cavalry leader Wade Hampton, who was wounded at First Bull Run, Seven Pines and Gettysburg.*

61

FREEMEN!
AVOID CONSCRIPTION!

The undersigned desires to raise a Company for the Confederate States service, and for that purpose I call upon the people of the Counties of Jefferson and Hawkins, Tenn., to meet promptly at Russellville, on SATURDAY, JULY 19th, 1862, and organize a Company.

By so doing you will avoid being taken as Conscripts, for that Act will now be enforced by order of the War Department. Rally, then, my Countrymen, to your Country's call.

S. M. DENNISON,
Of the Confederate States Army.

CHARLESTON, Tenn., JUNE 30, 1862.

Stuart bypassed Hagerstown, where the Army of the Potomac was 100,000 strong. Learning of Stuart's presence, McClellan sent Union Cavalry out after him, but the Federal detachments were so small and scattered as to be useless. On the night of 10 October, McClellan learned from Washington, rather than from his own cavalry, that Stuart had taken over Chambersburg, Pennsylvania, burning extensive Federal supplies and a machine shop and camping out in the town's streets. By the time McClellan heard the news Stuart was off on his circuit home, bringing with him a haul of captured horses.

On the banks of the Potomac, before the crossing, there was a particulary humiliating episode for the Union. Finding Federal infantry in force ready to resist his crossing, Rooney Lee sent word to the Yankees that Stuart was ready to charge (Stuart was actually some way behind) and they'd better surrender. The Federals didn't surrender, merely hightailed it. Stuart arrived and crossed his forces with little resistance. By 12 October the Rebel horsemen were back with Lee, having ridden 126 miles in four days, the last 24 hours covering 80 miles without a halt. They had commandeered 1200 horses, whipped every Yankee cavalry unit in their path and learned all Lee wanted to know about the Army of the Potomac. All this with three casualties. Thus the Chambersburg Raid became another element in the Stuart legend.

On 1 November Stuart and the Yankees tangled in a series of skirmishes at Snicker's Gap. It was an entirely typical example of the weakness and ineffectiveness of Federal Cavalry in those days. At one point Fitz Lee's brigade was fighting dismounted, so Union Cavalryman Alfred Pleasonton took them for part of Jackson's infantry. Pleasonton reported to McClellan that Jackson was there in force and too strong to attack; actually, the Federals outnumbered Stuart's men. Meanwhile, Stuart had found out what he wanted to know – that the Army of the Potomac was advancing deeper into Virginia.

By that point President Lincoln had finally had enough of General George McClellan, once dubbed 'the little Napoleon.' Despite his golden opportunity of the captured plans before Antietam, McClellan had not seriously damaged the enemy, and now he had let the Rebel Cavalry ride circles around him again. On 5 November Lincoln cashiered McClellan, which was certainly an appropriate move. But then, inexplicably, the president named as McClellan's replacement one of the most spectacularly inept military officers of all time, General Ambrose E Burnside (whose main contribution to history was the term 'sideburns,' named for his extravagant whiskers).

Lee and the Army of Northern Virginia shadowed Burnside's advance, keeping between the Northerners and Richmond. Finally, Lee settled into entrenchments at Fredericksburg, where he looked forward to a Federal offensive with manifest delight. Burnside made his attack on 13 December, throwing his entire army against Lee's lines. Lee had thought them impregnable, and so they proved: the Battle of Fredericksburg was one of the most disastrous of the war for the Union; the worst, too, in Burnside's career of debacles. On the slopes of Marye's Heights, behind Fredericksburg, the Union lost 13,000 casualties to the South's 5000.

During the Battle of Fredericksburg, Stuart's men had been positioned on Jackson's flank, which scarcely needed protecting, and so saw little action. But a few weeks later, Lee had need of their usual services as his army's eyes and spoilers. He sent the Cavalier on a series of raids on Burnside's communications. The last and largest of these operations was the Dumfries Raid of 26-31 December 1862. Riding with Stuart that week were the brigades of the two young Lees and Wade Hampton, and the horse artillery under John Pelham – 1800 in all. By now they were an experienced group, one schooled almost entirely in victories. With a certain grim humor, they had changed the words of an old tune of theirs: once it ran, 'If you want to have a good time, jine the cavalry'; now they sang, 'If you want to smell hell, jine the cavalry.'

After splashing across the Rappahannock River at Kelly's Ford on Christmas Day, Stuart's men spread out for some minor raiding. Stuart spent the 28th in skirmishes with Union Cavalry

near the village of Occoquan: in these the North lost 20 killed and wounded and 100 captured. Afterward, Stuart chased the Yankees out of their camps at Occoquan and burned everything he couldn't carry. Rejoined by his detachments, who brought their own captured wagons, the Rebels moved on to take a Federal telegraph station. There Stuart and his colonels listened in on an official communication from Washington detailing the dispositions being made against them. Stuart replied with a telegram of his own, complaining to the US Quartermaster-General about the poor quality of Federal mules – they could hardly pull the wagons he'd captured. By 31 December the Southern Cavalry were back with Lee in Fredericksburg, sporting some 200 prisoners and the same number of horses, 20 Federal wagons and a good haul of weapons and supplies. Southern losses had been one killed, 13 wounded and 13 missing. It had been another splendid week's work for the Cavalier and his men.

The year 1863 arrived with Southern hopes high in the Eastern theater (they had never been too high in the West, where an up-and-coming Federal general named Ulysses S Grant was swallowing enemy armies whole). By that year most cavalrymen in both armies had replaced their muzzle-loading rifles, almost useless on

Above: *The irascible Joseph (Fighting Joe) Hooker, who succeeded Burnside as commander of the Army of the Potomac.*

Opposite, top: *An 1862 recruiting poster for the Confederate States Army in Tennessee.*

Opposite, bottom: *Confederate General Robert E Lee, a brilliant tactician whose strategies were thwarted by Southern disunity in the conduct of the war.*

horseback, with shorter breechloading carbines. A few US Cavalrymen were already carrying Spencer repeating carbines, invented some years earlier but bull-headedly resisted by the Union command.

The year was to see a great number of other changes. Southern fortunes in the East had not yet peaked; they were about to do so, and then to decline once and for all. In January Lincoln replaced the hapless Ambrose Burnside with General Joseph E Hooker in command of the Army of the Potomac. Hooker spent a good deal of effort in expanding and revitalizing his cavalry, and the difference showed up soon enough: in March, Fitz Lee found himself under vigorous attack by a force of 3000 Union Cavalry near Culpeper, Virginia. Lee finally managed to repel the attack, but not before losing 133 men; among the dead was the great artillerist John Pelham, and that loss was irreplaceable. In his report, Stuart did not neglect to mention the new aggressiveness of the Union horsemen. He worried that it was an omen, and it was.

But large, important changes rarely happen suddenly; for a time, things were much as before. Hooker put the vast machinery and forces of his new Army of the Potomac, 134,000 strong, the greatest army ever seen on the American continent, on the move south toward Lee, proclaiming 'God have mercy on General Lee, for I will not.' Stuart scouted and screened the Confederate forces; as usual for Federal campaigns, Hooker came in blind, unable to get close enough to Lee to discover just how small the Confederate Army was (it was only 60,000). Hooker planned to leave a detachment at Fredericksburg to hold Lee there, then with the rest of his army to make a wide swing around the Rebels and come in from behind, dislodging them from their defenses and driving them back toward Richmond.

Hooker had neglected to put up a cavalry screen or to scout adequately, so on 31 March he was surprised to find Confederates waiting for him near a little wilderness clearing called Chancellorsville, just west of Fredericksburg. Lee, as usual, had heard all about the Federal movements from Stuart and correctly divined Hooker's intention. At the first brush with the enemy, the massive Union advance ground to a halt, and the Federals began to dig in. Then, riding at will around the periphery of the Union lines, Stuart made a critical discovery: the enemy's right flank was entirely unprotected, 'in the air.' Lee and Stonewall Jackson planned a little surprise for Joe Hooker.

Next day that surprise made its intended impression. Undetected by Federal Cavalry, Jackson led 25,000 men on a broad-daylight march right in front of the Union lines (the movement was screened by thick woods) and then struck and utterly routed the Union right flank. After a disastrous few hours for the North, darkness brought the Rebel advance to a halt.

It was on that victorious night of 2 May that the South's luck began to run out. Returning from a scouting foray in the dark, Stonewall Jackson was mortally wounded by his own men. A stunned Lee placed Jeb Stuart, who had never led infantry, in command of one wing of a two-pronged attack ordered for the next morning. The attack went off just as planned on 3 May, the Confederates driving the enemy before them, the two wings uniting at Hazel Grove near Chancellorsville. On 6 May the defeated and demoralized Hooker took his great Army of the Potomac and skedaddled across the Rappahannock. The triumvirate of Lee, Jackson and Stuart had executed one of the greatest masterpieces of strategy in military history, routing a foe over twice as large as their army. But in a few days, the indispensable Stonewall Jackson died, and with him the season of triumph for the Army of Northern Virginia.

Opposite: *General George Custer's cavalry brigade captures three Confederate guns near Culpeper, Virginia, in September 1863.*

Below: *General Thomas 'Stonewall' Jackson at First Bull Run.*

Of course, neither Robert E Lee nor his enemy yet knew that fact. What Lee did know after Chancellorsville was that his men had whipped the superbly outfitted Yankees once more. So again Lee made the fateful decision to invade the North, this time planning to go as far as Pennsylvania, in a campaign that would lead inexorably to the bloody fields of Gettysburg. Among Lee's reasons for the new offensive was to get the fighting out of his beloved Virginia; he also

Opposite: *Union Cavalry and Artillery take to the Yorktown Turnpike in pursuit of Confederate forces.*

hoped to draw Federal strength away from the South, where Grant was tightening the noose around Vicksburg and another Federal Army was threatening the vital rail center of Chattanooga. Lee put Stuart back in command of the cavalry and appointed the erratic Richard S Ewell to replace the irreplaceable Jackson. The Army of Northern Virginia seemed stronger and more confident than ever, 89,000 men of one of the greatest fighting forces that ever took the field. Stuart too was at his peak of strength and confidence, with 9000 men on horseback and 20 fieldpieces.

On 8 June 1863, Lee was concentrating at Culpeper, ready to send his army north across the Potomac into Maryland. Suspecting something was up, Joe Hooker sent 11,000 Federal Cavalrymen and infantry under Cavalry General Alfred Pleasonton to make a reconnaissance in force (Pleasonton was an old schoolmate of Stuart's at West Point). The result was simultaneously the first and the largest cavalry-only battle of the Civil War: Brandy Station.

At dawn on 9 June, Stuart's forces rested along the Rappahannock River between Brandy Station and Culpeper. Suddenly a column of 2000 Federal Cavalry under John Buford smashed into 'Grumble' Jones's men at Beverly Ford; six miles downstream another column, under John Gregg, crossed the river without resistance and converged in two divisions toward Stuart's camp.

In fierce fighting, Buford's riders killed 30 of Jones's men and sent the rest retreating. As would be the case during the whole battle, there were few infantrymen in the area and comparatively few shots to be heard; for one of the few times in the war nearly everyone had sabers in hand and fought with them. Downstream, Gregg's men ran into strong resistance from Wade Hampton, but within a short time the Federals had pushed back the forces of Hampton, Rooney Lee and Jones.

The battle raged up and down the river. A couple of Federal riders later recalled the style of the fighting: 'Two fellows put at me. The first one fired at me and missed. Before he could again cock his revolver I succeeded in closing with him. My saber took him just in the neck, and must have cut the jugular. The blood gushed out in a black-looking stream; he gave a horrible yell.' Another remembered, 'The cavalry were fighting over and around the guns.... There was one rebel, on a splendid horse, who sabered three gunners while I was chasing him. He wheeled in and out – would dart away and then come sweeping back and cut down another man. He got off without a scratch.' On the other side, a Confederate rider took note of the new effectiveness of the Northern riders: 'The improvement in the cavalry of the enemy became painfully apparent. They were much better provided with long-range carbines than our cavalry, which gave them an advantage dismounted.'

SHERIDAN'S FINAL CHARGE AT WINCHESTER

Above: *Sheridan's last charge at Winchester.*

Left: *Reader's painting Rebels Riding into Line of Battle.*

Above: *A Ranger of the 8th Texas Cavalry, CSA.*

Left: *The Battle of Winchester (Opequan).*

Above: *Artillery going into action on south bank of the Rappahannock River, Virginia, 4 June 1863.*

Right: *Charge of the 6th New York Cavalry, led by Major William P Hall, at Brandy Station, Virginia, 11 October 1863.*

Right: *General Buford's cavalry charges near Beverley Ford, on the Rappahannock, in an engraving from a sketch by A R Waud.*

For the first time, Stuart saw his men scattered and thrown back by Federals. Patiently, he began to organize his forces, sending Hampton's men against Gregg's flanks. About this time, Rooney Lee was seriously wounded; he was to be out of the war for over a year. Finally, the dash and experience of the Southern Cavalrymen began to prevail. Gregg was driven out of Brandy Station, Pleasonton ordered a pullback after hearing a mistaken report of Rebel infantry approaching and the Federal Cavalry rode back across the Rappahannock.

Union losses were considerably worse than Confederate – 936 to Stuart's 523 – and the South held the field. The Southern horse had prevailed again, but not with the ease of previous engagements. This time the Union had stood and fought hard: the Northern Cavalry might not always win, but they were never again to be humiliated. Even at the time this change was clear to everyone on both sides. A Southern officer later wrote of the Battle of Brandy Station, 'One result of incalculable importance certainly did follow this battle ..., it *made* the Federal cavalry. Up to that time confessedly inferior to the Southern horsemen, they gained on this day that confidence in themselves and in their commanders which enabled them to contest so fiercely the subsequent battlefields of June, July, and October.' Moreover, Pleasonton's operation had accomplished just what it was supposed to: he reported to Hooker that Lee was definitely heading north on what appeared to be another invasion, and Hooker began moving the Army of the Potomac to shadow the Confederates, staying between the enemy and Washington.

There was yet another unexpected benefit to the North from that day at Brandy Station – the battle was perceived in the South as a humiliation for Jeb Stuart. For the first time, the Southern papers criticized him in their customary vitriolic terms. The Cavalier seethed with resentment, looking for a way to get his revenge with another bold stroke.

As the two armies moved north, circling Washington, a series of cavalry skirmishes developed. On 17 June at Aldie, Virginia, Federal Cavalry under Pleasonton and Judson

Kilpatrick fell on Longstreet's cavalry screen, making several spirited attacks before being driven away. Later the same day, a mixed force of Federal Cavalry, infantry, and artillery drove Stuart's men out of the town of Middleburg; Stuart pulled back into a defensive position and the Yankees withdrew. Two days later the Federals renewed their pressure on Stuart, trying to drive him back into the safety of Lee's army. Divisions of Union Cavalry under Gregg and Buford, with infantry, drove Stuart out of his position near Middleburg, and the Confederate brigades of Hampton and Robertson pulled back to Upperville with other forces driven there by Buford. A considerable wrangle developed, with Kilpatrick's Federals making two charges and breaking into the Rebel lines at Upperville. Finally, Stuart had to pull out of the town into defensive positions at Ashby's Gap.

Altogether, those three days of skirmishing added up to no small engagement; in them the North lost 613 casualties, the South 510. It was clear now that the new Federal confidence seen at Brandy Station was no accident: the pains Hooker had taken with his cavalry were paying off. Inconclusive as they were, these skirmishes brought a most important benefit for the North – they kept Stuart at a distance from the Army of the Potomac. For the first time, Lee was marching blind into enemy territory. Thus the tables were turned: now Hooker knew more or less where Lee was, and Lee had little idea that the Federal Army was shadowing him. Then Jeb Stuart came up with an idea that was to make things still more precarious for the South.

Probably still smarting from his humiliation at Brandy Station, Stuart proposed to Lee that his cavalry repeat their old stunt of riding around the enemy. Responding to the proposal, Lee issued an ambiguously phrased order that stated, 'You had better move over to Fredericks-town. You will, however, be able to judge whether you can pass around their army without hindrance ... and cross the river east of the mountains.' It is not clear, then, whether Lee was fully approving the Cavalier's plan; it is certain that neither of them had any idea how spread out the Army of the Potomac was, and

Above: *Trooper of the 6th New York Cavalry Regiment.*

thus how far the Confederate horse would have to ride to 'pass around their army without hindrance.'

This point of the war was the most critical for the South, and its outcome resulted from a confluence of weaknesses that had existed in the Army of Northern Virginia all along. These included Lee's poor logistics, which resulted in a perpetually hungry and ill-clad army (another reason for Lee's invasion was to forage for food in Pennsylvania, and it was to be a matter of shoes that triggered the battle of Gettysburg). Another weakness was Lee's habit of giving vague and sometimes confusing orders, and a third was Stuart's penchant for boldness and drama whether or not the situation called for it.

Stuart and his men rode out on 24 June. They were not to rejoin Lee until 2 July, by which day the South was in the midst of losing both the battle and the war. Between those two dates, the Southern Army marched deep into enemy territory with the whole Union Army between them and their cavalry – their eyes.

The Cavalier's riders began skirting the Army of the Potomac, meanwhile skirmishing with the Federal Cavalry screen. At Rockville, Stuart hit a Federal supply line, capturing 125 wagons and many prisoners (the latter naturally slowing him down). On 27 June at Fairfax, Virginia, Wade Hampton's men charged some New York

cavalry and captured nearly the whole outfit. By 28 June Stuart was some 15 miles outside Washington, with the Army of the Potomac exactly between him and Lee. On that day the Federal Army got yet another commander. Since Hooker's humiliation at Chancellorsville, leaders in Washington had been jockeying for the right political moment to replace him. Finally, virtually on the eve of battle, the choleric and stubborn George G Meade became the fifth commander of the Army of the Potomac in a year's time. Hearing the news, Lee accurately prophesied: 'General Meade will make no mistake on my front.' The Army of the Potomac finally had a commander who would let them show their mettle.

Detouring farther and farther east to get around the enemy, Stuart found himself under surprise attack in the late afternoon of 29 June at Westminster, Maryland. There the outnumbered Federals charged gallantly but were soon repulsed. Next day Stuart found a body of Union

Above; *The Battle of Chancellorsville.*

Cavalry at Hanover, Pennsylvania, and charged them; the Federals broke and then re-formed, mounting a counterattack that routed the Confederates in turn. This time the Yankees very nearly bagged a big prize indeed – Stuart found himself surrounded and escaped at the last second by jumping his horse over a wide ditch. At the end of the engagement, there were 215 Federal and 117 Southern casualties. Burdened by a column of captured prisoners and wagons (whose Yankee drivers were in no hurry), Stuart struggled back, looking for Lee. He wasted the bulk of 1 July in sporadic shelling of the town of Carlisle, Pennsylvania, whose militia had refused to surrender. Receiving word of Lee's location at last, he hurried back toward a town called Gettysburg. That day the greatest battle ever seen on American soil had begun without Jeb Stuart.

The battle had spluttered into life when a force of Rebels marched toward Gettysburg to see if they could find shoes – many Confederate soldiers were barefoot. West of town they had run into a detachment of John Buford's cavalry, who dismounted and peppered the Rebels with their Spencer repeating carbines while the Federal infantry moved up. Piece by piece, both armies began pitching units into the battle until a gigantic engagement, planned by neither side, was raging west of Gettysburg. The first day of fighting went well for the South; Union forces were driven back across the town to defensive positions on Cemetery Ridge and the flanking hills. But those Union positions, arrived at by accident after a rout, were to spell disaster for the Confederacy.

On the second day of the battle (2 July), Stuart's men were too exhausted to fight. In the infantry actions of that day, Lee's attacks went off haltingly and piecemeal; by a thread, Union General Meade's army held its line. Next day Lee decided to try and smash the Union center by an infantry charge of 15,000 men. That effort, known to history as Pickett's Charge, was

doomed from the outset by the impenetrable Union position on Cemetery Ridge. But while that charge, the high-water mark of the Confederacy, was taking its tragic course, there were separate cavalry battles on both flanks, battles that in some ways were just as critical to the outcome.

While Lee's grand charge was moving on the Federal center, Stuart had been ordered to cut Meade's communications on the Union right. If this were accomplished, Meade would have to draw off infantry to protect his rear. Confidently, the brigades of Wade Hampton and Fitz Lee, still schooled largely in victory, moved to the attack. Opposing them were the Federal Cavalry of D M Gregg, J I Gregg, J B McIntosh and a young and impetuous general named George Armstrong Custer.

The Federals watched the Southern horsemen approaching in close columns of squadrons, as if on parade. Then Union artillery belched a storm of double canister into the Rebel line, turning its front rank into a mass of floundering men and horses. The Southern officers shouted 'Keep to your sabers, men!' and ordered the charge,

straight toward a Michigan outfit. At the head of the Blue cavalry rode General Custer, who watched the enemy galloping toward him for a moment before standing in his stirrups and shouting 'Come on, you Wolverines!' The two lines crashed together with the sound, one observer recalled, of a great tree falling. Quickly the fight broke up into a confused melee of individual struggles, charge and countercharge, units fighting sometimes mounted and sometimes dismounted. Wade Hampton went down with a saber cut on his head. As the hours wore on and his men fell in dozens, Jeb Stuart anxiously awaited word that Pickett's charge had broken through the Federal center. The word never came.

Stuart's battle died down inconclusively in the late afternoon; he had not achieved his objective of cutting Meade's communications. Over on the Union right, a foolhardy charge by Judson Kilpatrick's Union Cavalry had been cut to pieces by Southern infantry. Finally, Stuart's men gave up and rode to the rear. The greatest and most terrible battle on American soil was over.

Above: *Panicked and wounded horses struggle in their traces at the Battle of Gettysburg.*

Opposite: *Major General George A Custer (left) with General Alfred Pleasanton. Custer's Civil War record was far more impressive than his subsequent role on the Western frontier.*

For the Army of Northern Virginia it was, at last, a day of complete and unmitigated defeat. And partial blame for that defeat must be laid at the door of Jeb Stuart, whose raid had blinded Lee at the most critical moment of the war. Now it was to be the turn of the Union Cavalrymen, and especially of a little Irishman named Philip Sheridan.

Lee's stricken forces pulled back into Virginia. They were to go on fighting for nearly two years more, but never again with such strength and confidence. The South was running out of soldiers and its cavalry out of horses. While Lee was losing at Gettysburg, Grant was seeing victory in his long campaign against Vicksburg, Mississippi. In both the Eastern and Western theaters the war had turned against the Confederacy that July, and it would never really turn back. Jeb Stuart and his cavalrymen still had much hard riding to do, including the Wilderness Campaign that was followed by Spotsylvania, but now it was too late for the Cavalier or anyone else to stop the Federal juggernaut. All Stuart's riding would only bring him closer to a place called Yellow Tavern.

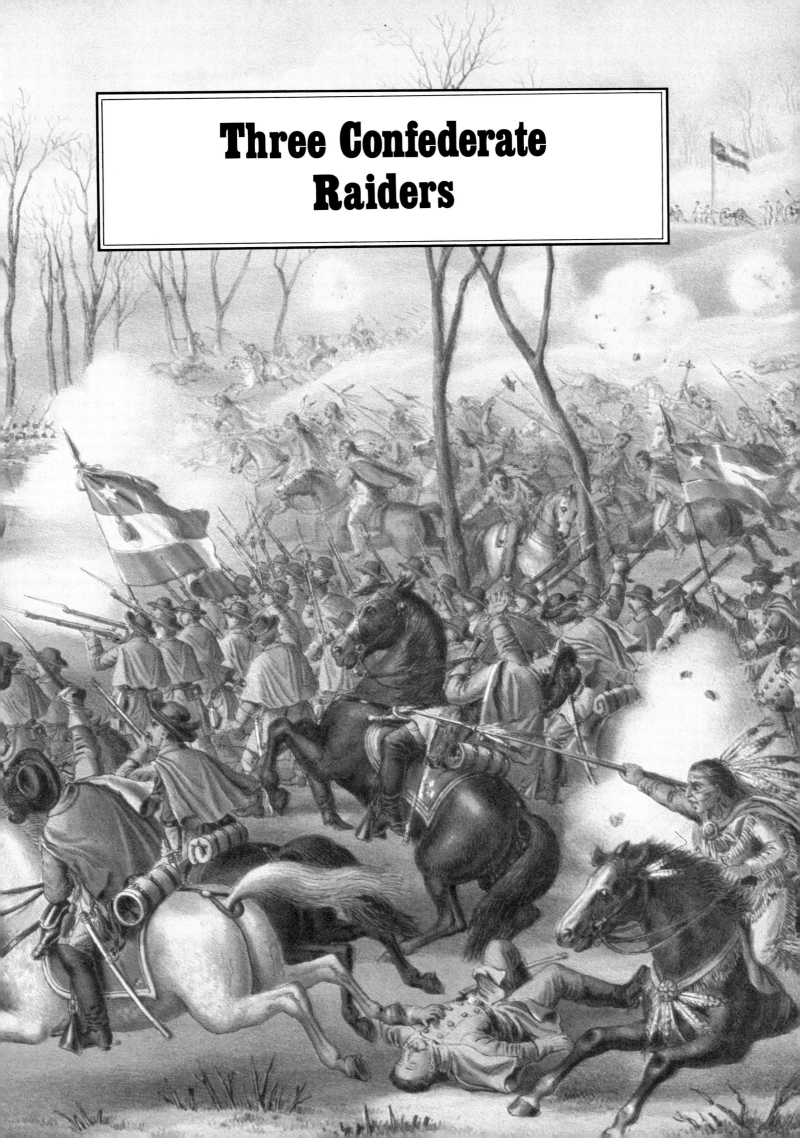

Three Confederate Raiders

Previous pages: *The Battle of Pea Ridge, Arkansas, March 1862.*

Left: *Colonel John S Mosby, who carved out 'Mosby's Confederacy' with his raiders.*

The highly irregular career of Southern irregular John Singleton Mosby may be said to have begun with a stint in jail, where he landed after shooting a fellow University of Virginia student during a fracas. In jail Mosby began reading law with his defense counsel and after his release went into legal practice. When the Civil War broke out, Mosby, then 28, joined a Virginia cavalry outfit and from there hitched up with Jeb Stuart's command, for which he acted as a guide on Stuart's first ride around McClellan and on a number of other operations.

Too restless and independent to be content with riding in Jeb Stuart's shadow, Mosby gained permission in January of 1863 to form a group of raiders to operate in Virginia. It was then that he became the Mosby known to history – the most successful guerrilla fighter of the war. He and his men were officially dubbed Partisan Rangers and given formal status in the Confederate Army – this in an effort, usually successful, to keep them from being hung as spies and looters when captured. But from the beginning the group functioned informally, free of the usual military protocol – only Mosby was ever saluted or addressed by his rank, uniforms were *ad hoc* and aside from a great deal of shooting practice, there was never any drill. The band soon became known to friend and foe alike as 'Mosby's Irregulars,' and their usual territory of operations in Virginia was 'Mosby's Confed-

Above: *Union Cavalry scouting near Fairfax Courthouse, Virginia, after a skirmish that saw 30 of their number captured or killed.*

Opposite: *Mosby's raiders capture and loot a Union wagon train carrying supplies, as seen in an 1863 issue of* Harper's Weekly.

eracy.' Wearing a feathered hat second only in fame to Jeb Stuart's, Mosby himself was dubbed 'the Grey Ghost.' In effect, he and his Irregulars had themselves a nice private war for the duration; in the end they were never captured and never surrendered, but simply disbanded and melted back into the countryside. In this they were the closest thing in the Civil War to the band led by Francis Marion, the Swamp Fox of the Revolution.

Like Marion's men, Mosby's raiders galloped out on hit-and-run missions, each man armed with two or three six-shooters, and spent most of their nonworking time at home or as guests of friendly farmers. Thus, in contrast to most Confederate soldiers, they ate well throughout the war. Their accoutrements were similarly luxurious; in later years an old Irreular recalled, 'We had ups and downs; but after our successful raids we were the best dressed, best equipped, and best mounted Command in the Confederate Army.... Union army sutlers supplied us with a varied assortment of luxuries, and I cannot recall an instance when we rejected what they had on hand or when we threatened to take our trade to some competitor.' Indeed, the primary draw for joining on with Mosby was the food and the loot. Foraging from civilians was forbidden, but anything Yankee was fair game, and after a raid the haul was divided among all (a captured Union payroll once provided $2100 in crisp new greenbacks for each raider).

During their first couple of months, the Ir-

regulars worked in obscurity, often functioning as an advance for Jeb Stuart and stealing Yankee horses for his cavalry. But in March of 1863, Mosby and his men hit the headlines North and South with their raid on Fairfax Court House. There, on the night of 7 March, Mosby and 39 partisans threaded their way between Federal guards, cut the telegraph lines and then transformed themselves into a 'Federal' patrol. Asleep in his bed, Union general Edwin H Stoughton was shaken awake by a slap on his bare behind and found himself confronting a group of strangers. Stoughton demanded to know the meaning of this, and got his reply from Mosby himself: 'It means, sir, that Stuart's cavalry are in possession of this place, and you are a prisoner.' With Stoughton and 31 other captured Federals in tow, plus 58 horses, the raiders slipped quietly back out of Union lines. Their only close call came when a Union colonel challenged them from an open window; seeing enemy soldiers materialize at his door, the colonel hightailed it out the back 'in a nude state' and hid under the privy. No doubt Jeb Stuart roared with his famous laughter when he heard the report.

From then on, Mosby's name would frequent the headlines. Under the twin lures of loot and adventure, hundreds flocked to join his band, somtimes deserting other Confederate outfits to do so. Eventually, Mosby mustered some 1000 men under the designation of the 43rd Virginia Cavalry Battalion, but most of his raids used

fewer than 300, and Irregulars they remained.

When in June 1863 Lee needed information about Hooker and the Army of the Potomac, Mosby got his news by the simple expedient of riding through the enemy's camps. Later in the year Stuart sent Mosby to operate against a rail crossing at Warrenton Junction, behind Union lines in Virginia. The Irregulars burned all the culverts and trestles they could get to, then headed for Catlett's Station with a captured howitzer. Next day they cut the telegraph wires, pulled a rail from the track, aimed the howitzer down the line, and awaited developments. When the Federal train appeared, it ran off the track at top speed where the rail had been removed. The Federal guard of 200 men was sent on their way by a round of grapeshot from the howitzer. Finally, the Federals pitched into the tiny group of Irregulars and chased them away, but the Union suffered 12 casualties to Mosby's one loss.

During Sheridan's Shenandoah Valley Campaign of 1864, Grant, tired of his operations being bedeviled by Mosby's band, ordered the Irregulars hanged without trial if captured. The order was followed only once, by George Custer, who captured six of Mosby's men, hanged a couple and shot the others. Mosby sent word to the Federals that he'd retaliate eye for eye, then hanged six Yankees. Thereafter, Grant's order was ignored.

So it went through the long months of the war, the Grey Ghost and his partisans remaining

supreme in Mosby's Confederacy to the end. During the Wilderness Campaign, Grant diverted a good number of men in efforts to bring Mosby to bay; they never succeeded, though Irregular operations were reduced after Sheridan's campaign in the Shenandoah. As noted earlier, Mosby and his Rangers were never caught and never surrendered, but ended their

Top: *Battle of the Wilderness 5–6 May 1864.*

Above: *Todd's Tavern – Sheridan's cavalry vs Stuart's. Six days later, Stuart would die at the age of 31.*

It Went Against Us, *by Samuel J Reader, one of many American artists who were inspired by the immense national tragedy that was the Civil War.*

Right: *Reader's depiction of a charging Confederate horseman titled* Kill the Yanks – Shoot Them!

private war on their own terms. Later a former Union general was to call Mosby's operations 'the only perfect success in the Southern army.'

In his long postwar career Mosby remained unpredictable, not least in his friendships. In his *Memoirs,* U S Grant wrote of the man he had once ordered hanged: 'Since the close of the war, I have come to know Colonel Mosby personally and somewhat intimately. He is a different man entirely from what I had supposed. . . . He is able and thoroughly honest and truthful.' In fact, Mosby was an active Republican canvasser in Virginia when Grant ran for president. He was rewarded by President Grant with an ambassadorship to Hong Kong. After working in a series of government posts, including the Department of Justice, the Grey Ghost died in Washington in 1916. From beginning to end, from jail to the Justice Department, Mosby was one of a kind.

When the war broke out, John Hunt Morgan was the successful proprietor of a hemp and woolen mill in Lexington, Kentucky, and a former volunteer in the Mexican War. After some hesitation, Kentucky elected to stay in the Union despite its slaveholding status. But Morgan, without hesitation, cast his own lot with the South and took a company of militia, which he had founded earlier, to join Albert Sidney Johnston's Confederate Army. Throughout his ensuing career as a raider, he would command mainly Kentuckians. As with Mosby, Morgan's men eventually included deserters

Top: *Morgan's raid on Paris, Kentucky, where 'contributions' were demanded from the inhabitants.*

Above: *Morgan and his men on the march. They were feared and respected for their hard-riding raids.*

Right: *Before the Civil War, John Hunt Morgan was a successful Kentucky businessman who led a militia troop called the Lexington rifles.*

A detail of the Battle of Shiloh from a painting by Alonzo Chappell – Union soldiers struggle to recapture a gun.

from other Confederate Armies who were attracted by the prospect of adventure and loot.

In the Battle of Shiloh (April 1862) in Tennessee, Morgan commanded the Kentucky Squadron of Cavalry as its colonel. Already the soldiers in his division were calling themselves Morgan's Men. It was after that battle that he made his first raid, taking 325 men on a small but successful jaunt into Tennessee, where they captured and burned much Union matériel. Soon Morgan had a mounted regiment and prepared to make a career as a guerrilla fighter. In July of 1862 Morgan mounted his first major operation. With 800 men, he left Knoxville and headed for Kentucky, capturing a post of Yankee cavalry at Tomkinsville and a couple of Union depots. He continued on to Cynthiana, where he got into a sharp engagement with some Unionist Kentucky militia and pulled back. By the time he returned to Tennessee, he and his men had ridden over 1000 miles in 24 days, captured and paroled 1200 prisoners and lost fewer than 100 men. He had also upset a planned Federal invasion of Chattanooga and made himself a permanent headache to Federal strategists in the vicinity.

In most of his campaigns, Morgan's soldiers fought with revolvers on horseback, but more often dismounted to use their rifles. Morgan was old-fashioned enough to prefer muzzle-loading rifles, claiming that with them soldiers were less inclined to waste their shots. In practice this was manifestly not true: statistically speaking, during the war it took about one man's weight in lead to kill one enemy, regardless of the type of weapon – thus the quantity of fire was more significant than the quality. Like Jeb Stuart, Morgan always brought along horse artillery on his operations.

In October, following Confederate General Bragg's abortive invasion of Kentucky, Morgan went out with 1800 men on his second big raid into his home state. Virtually without opposition, his brigade rode all over Kentucky capturing Federal outposts and tearing up the railroads. At the end of the year, he operated against Federal communications and supplies in Tennessee, destroying some $2,000,000 worth of Federal property. With these successes under his belt, Morgan got very ambitious indeed – too ambitious, as it turned out: he decided to invade the North, to raid Ohio and Indiana.

The ostensible strategic purpose of this raid was to relieve pressure on Confederate Armies in the South after the fall of Vicksburg, which was then imminent. Among other worrisome problems, a Union Army under William S Rosecrans was heading toward Chattanooga. Ohio was also the most active area for Northern Democrats sympathetic to the South, who were

The Battle of Chattanooga:
General Thomas's charge
near Orchard Knob, 24
November 1863.

Thomas Nast's view of Confederate raiders laying waste a Western town, published in Harper's Weekly *in 1864.*

known as Copperheads; Morgan hoped to stir up these and other Southern sympathizers in the state. The raiders began in good form by chasing a Union Army away from Knoxville, after which Morgan and his 2500 men rode on into Kentucky. Soon they were running into more resistance than they were used to; trying to cross the Green River into Indiana on 4 July, Morgan's forces were repulsed by a fort containing 400 Michigan soldiers under the command of General Henry M Judah. Morgan and his men moved on, raiding and looting as they went (including robbing a bank). They got away from Lebanon, Kentucky, with 400 Federal prisoners and a considerable haul of captured supplies. On 7 July Morgan used two commandeered steamers to take his force across the Ohio River into Indiana.

Riding and raiding most of the day and into the night, Morgan's column headed northwest, brushing local militia out of the way (the Indiana Home Guard suffered 360 casualties, 345 of them missing in action). Confederate saddles spilled over with captured goods. (For some reason no officer could figure out, the favored loot was calico – most of Morgan's raiders carried massive bolts of the cloth on their horses.) Panic spread like wildfire among the civilian populations of Indiana and Ohio, who felt themselves at the mercy of an unpredictable enemy.

In short, things were going well for the raiders early in the campaign. Morgan had with him an expert telegraph wiretapper who kept him abreast of Union efforts to stop him and in return sent phony messages to Federal commanders; one of the messages falsely warned that Nathan Bedford Forrest, a name feared at least as much as Morgan's, was coming to reinforce the raiders. At this, the Union command in the area sank into utter confusion. By 13 July the raiders were in Ohio, still riding day and night. However, the rigors of the campaign were taking their toll on horses and men alike; the column was now reduced to about 2000, and exhausted mounts had to be exchanged for commandeered horses, some of them unshod. Learning that Federal troops under generals Judah and Burnside were waiting for him in Cincinnati, Morgan took his men through the suburbs of the city in pitch darkness. During the night, riders in his trailing columns had to stop at intersections, get down on hands and knees and, since there were hoofprints going in every direction, try to figure out which trail had the freshest horse slaver and manure so they could follow their leading column (as good an example as any of the often-unromantic side of soldiering in those days).

By the time Morgan and his men made it to Williamsburg, Ohio, they had ridden and

Left: *John Morgan's Raiders charge an impromptu barricade in a woodland attack.*

marched 90 miles in 35 hours and were beyond exhaustion. They rested there a few hours before pulling wearily away. It was at that point that Morgan's luck began to run out. He was harassed by state militia and encountered stiff Federal resistance at Pomeroy, in southeast Ohio. On the 18th the raiders stopped in Buffington; Morgan had intended to recross the Ohio River at the town but found some Federals forted up and ready to resist. Next morning the Rebels mounted an attack on the fort only to find the defenders gone. However, the Yankees turned up again soon enough – some 10,000 of Judah's troops, supported by gunboats on the river, attacked Morgan, boxed his force into a valley, and whipped him badly. About 120 of the raiders were killed and 700 captured. With 300 men Morgan retreated north toward Pennsylvania. His rearguard, who were out of ammunition, stood off the pursuing Federals with swords.

With Judah's Federals in hot pursuit, Morgan and his remaining men somehow made it some 200 miles to the northeast before being brought to bay. Near New Lisbon, 10 miles from the Pennsylvania border, Morgan and 365 officers and men surrendered. It had been the best of raids and the worst of raids. The Confederates had accomplished a phenomenal feat of endurance, averaging 21 hours a day in the saddle since entering Ohio. On the other hand, their entire force had been annihilated on a mission of dubious value. As a later commentator wrote, 'This reckless adventure . . . deprived [Morgan] of his well-earned reputation.'

It was nearly the end of Morgan's contributions to the Confederate cause, but not quite. In November 1863 Morgan and a few of his officers tunnelled out of a Federal prison in Columbus, Ohio, and made their way back to Kentucky. They were received with general rejoicing, and in 1864 Morgan was given command of the District of Southwestern Virginia. Dozens of his old raiders began filtering back to join him. After

fighting an inconclusive battle in Wythe County, Virginia, Morgan tried another raid into Kentucky with 1000 men (400 were on foot for lack of horses). For a while Morgan seemed to have regained his old dash; he outrode Union detachments in the hills of Appalachia and began cutting railroads and telegraph lines and burning bridges. But on 9 June Union General Stephen Burbridge jumped Morgan's column and repulsed it with heavy losses. The Confederates retreated to Lexington, where Burbridge trounced them again the next day. Desperately, Morgan straggled on with his remaining raiders, who began looting like common bandits.

On 4 September Federal General A C Gillem surrounded Morgan's last contingent in their bivouac at Greeneville, Tennessee. The Rebels tried to break out and 100 were killed. Among the dead was John Hunt Morgan. He had made a brilliant start in the raiding business, but his ambitions had outrun achievable goals – unlike Mosby, whose realism made him the more successful raider. On the other hand, maybe Morgan was simply unlucky – luck playing a far greater role in military matters than is usually admitted. In any case, by the time of Morgan's death the war was virtually over.

Above: *Confederate cavalry leader John Mosby reviews his horsemen, still 600 strong, on 21 April 1865.*

85

Below: Nathan Bedford Forrest, whom Confederate General J E Johnston would describe as the greatest soldier of the Civil War.

There is no doubt that Nathan Bedford Forrest was one of the great military geniuses of the war; the question is, where did his genius come from? Not only did Forrest have no military training (the majority of the war's officers on both sides were West Pointers), he had hardly any schooling at all, and his spelling was as rough as his speech. Born into a poor white family, Forrest went on to a business life that included slave dealing (and for all their willingness to fight and die for slavery, most Southerners looked down on the slave trade itself). By the time the war broke out, Forrest had raised himself quite high by his bootstraps, having progressed from selling slaves to selling real estate in Memphis. As Forrest later said, 'I went into the army worth a million and a half dollars and came out a beggar.' The most famous quote attributed to him, however, is of doubtful authenticity but has survived as a succinct summary of military strategy: 'Git thar fustest with the mostest.' Throughout his military career, Forrest was to show his genius mainly in his ability to maneuver inferior forces into local superiority over the enemy.

With the coming of the war, Forrest raised a mounted regiment out of his own pocket and became its colonel.

His men were outfitted with pistols and shotguns rather than sabers and usually dismounted to fight. Soon Forrest was in charge of eight companies, some 650 men. They saw little action until the end of 1861, when he and his forces routed some Union Cavalry in Sacramento, Kentucky, where Forrest maneuvered the enemy into defeat, showing for the first time his intuitive tactical skills. In February of 1862, Forrest's division was inside Fort Donelson on the Mississippi during Grant's siege. The fort had been starved out, and the Confederate generals voted to surrender; Forest refused to surrender and got permission to try to fight his way out. Somehow he led a column of 200 men through the Federal lines to safety: these were

the only troops Grant did not capture.

Two months later Forrest was fighting Grant again as commander of a regiment at the Battle of Shiloh in Tennessee. Placed in reserve, Forrest moved up on his own tack during the first day's fighting to help wipe out a pocket of Union resistance in the Hornet's Nest. That night he tried to convince his superiors to attack the Federal reinforcements that were arriving steadily; the generals refused, and next day Grant used those reinforcements to send the Rebels into retreat after their first day's victory. That day Forrest's regiment fought dismounted in the middle of the Confederate lines, then covered the rear during the retreat. His regiment broke up Sherman's advance with their shotguns, chasing the bluecoats back to the main line. It was Sherman's first encounter with the man destined to be his *bête noire*. Finally, Forrest charged the Yankees singlehandedly and was badly wounded; in fact, it was declared a fatal wound, but he was back in action three weeks later.

Forrest was made a brigadier general in the summer of 1862, with command of 1400 troops. On 13 July he led them against a large Federal depot at Murfreesboro, Tennessee; half the Federals ended up as casualties, the other 1200 as prisoners. It was the first of many raids, most of them in Tennessee, for Forrest and his 'critter

company,' actions that would make life considerably less pleasant and more dangerous for Union soldiers in the South.

In the spring of 1863 a Union Army under Rosecrans was deadlocked with the forces of Confederate General Braxton Bragg in middle Tennessee. The raids of Forrest and Morgan had made the Federal position tenuous. To deal with this, Federal Colonel Abel Streight was sent out with a mule-mounted command to draw off the Rebel raiders. Streight's column headed into Alabama in mid-April. Soon Forrest was on their trail, telling his men to 'Shoot at everything blue and keep up the scare.' The Rebels did so, and Streight found Forrest's men apparently as thick as the trees. The Federal column limped east across Alabama, fighting incessantly. Finally, on 3 May, Streight gave in to the inevitable and met with Forrest under truce to discuss surrender terms. During the conversation Forrest had his forces, which were about a third of the Federals', circle around and around a hill until Streight exclaimed, 'Name of God! How many guns have you got? There's fifteen I've counted already.' There were, in fact, two cannons. When Streight found out he had surrendered 1466 prisoners to a force of 500, the Union colonel was outraged and demanded that Forrest give him back his men and fight it out.

General Ulysses S Grant
leads the charge at the
Battle of Shiloh, 6–7 April
1862.

Right: *Jefferson Davis, President of the Confederate States of America, looked like an aristocratic planter, but came from a farming family of modest means. He attended West Point at the same time as Robert E Lee.*

'Ah, Colonel,' Forrest drawled, 'all is fair in love and war, you know.'

Nemesis that he was to his enemies, Forrest had nemeses of his own – namely, the Confederate command structure, which never seemed to recognize his brilliance. Confederate President Jefferson Davis had a remarkable talent for holding down good generals and promoting bad ones. Though Forrest was spared the fate of first-rate generals like Beauregard and J E Johnston, who were ignored for much of the war, his superiors had the habit of rewarding his successes by taking his outfit away from him. Still, Forrest always ended up with another command, and always led it to victory. Given Forrest's fiery temper, there were inevitable problems with subordinates as well, one of whom shot Forrest during an argument in June 1863. Forrest grabbed the officer's pistol hand, held it fast while he opened a penknife with his teeth and stabbed his assailant mortally. In the fall of that year, Forrest watched his superior Braxton Bragg win the Battle of Chickamauga and then let the Yankees get away to Chattanooga without a chase.

In a perfect fury, Forrest screamed at Bragg, 'You commenced your cowardly . . . persecution after Shiloh, because I reported to Richmond facts, while you reported damned lies. You robbed me of my command that I armed and equipped from the enemies. You are a coward and a damned scoundrel. You may as well not issue any more orders to me, for I will not obey them. For some reason Bragg did not have Forrest called up for insubordination – perhaps because Forrest was irreplaceable, perhaps because Bragg suspected he was right. In any case, Forrest went raging off to Richmond, where Jefferson Davis gave him another independent command.

On 12 April 1864, Forrest and his division surrounded Union Fort Pillow, which lay on the Mississippi in Tennessee. Having established his men so they could attack the fort without coming under fire themselves, Forrest asked for surrender, but the Union commander declined. The ensuing Rebel attack was swift and successful, with only 90 casualties. But what happened next was as inglorious as anything in the war. Half the Union defenders of the fort were black. During the action over 200 of these black soldiers died, more than twice the number of whites.

The details remain shrouded in mystery, but it seems most likely that the blacks were deliberately slaughtered, many of them after surrender.

Northern survivors reported the Confederates screaming 'No quarter! Kill the damned niggers; shoot them down!' After the battle Forrest wrote in a letter, 'The river was dyed with the blood of the slaughtered for two hundred yards ... it is hoped that these facts will demonstrate to the Northern people that Negro soldiers cannot cope with Southerners.' Despite official Southern denials, the North erupted into accusations of massacre. History has largely supported those accusations.

Thereafter, Forrest made a specialty of hounding the supply lines of Union General W T Sherman, who was pushing south toward Atlanta in the spring and summer of 1864. With increasing frustration, Sherman sent forces after Forrest, only to have them return empty-handed. Meanwhile, the Federal supply line became longer and more vulnerable by the day. At the beginning of June, Sherman was howling 'That devil Forrest must be hunted down and killed if it costs ten thousand lives and bankrupts the Federal treasury!' Sherman sent out a detachment of 3000 cavalry, 4800 infantry and 18 cannons under General S D Sturgis to do the hunting and killing.

As always, Forrest did not wait for the enemy but took the offensive himself, though he had available only 4713 men and 12 cannons. Learning of Sturgis's approach to Brice's Cross Roads

General Grant was widely criticized for the heavy Union casualties at the Battle of Shiloh, but Lincoln came to his defense. 'I can't spare this man,' said the President. 'He fights.'

Right: *A parley between Generals Sherman and Joseph E Johnston during the last year of the war.*

Below: Confederates under Nathan B Forrest storm Fort Pillow in April 1864. Colonel Robert McCulloch commanded the left wing of the Confederate force, seen here.

in Mississippi, Forrest moved his forces up fast and beat Sturgis to the crossroads. On 10 June Forrest was met at the crossroads by General Benjamin Grierson's cavalry, 3200 strong; at that point Forrest had some 900 men in position and his artillery was eight miles back. Nonetheless, Forrest dismounted his troops and sent them forward to attack, making them as visible as possible. The bluff worked: Grierson did not press forward to find how thin the enemy line was. After falling back and finding the Yankees did not advance, Forrest ordered another bluffing attack. Finally, the Confederate artillery and troops began to arrive. When the main Federal column pulled in, exhausted from marching in the fierce early afternoon heat, they found themselves under attack in earnest. With no more than 1700 men actively engaged, Forrest by then had broken through Grierson's center while immobilizing his flanks. By five o'clock in the afternoon, the Confederates were crumpling the flanks of the Federal battle line. At that point the Union forces fell into utter panic and fled; Forrest chased them the rest of the night and next day. With less than half the Federals' numbers, he had beaten them decisively and captured 250 wagons and ambulances, 18 cannons, 5000 rifles, massive quantities of ammunition and the entire baggage train. Sturgis lost 227 killed, 394 wounded and 1623 captured; Southern losses numbered about 492 in all. The Battle of Brice's Cross Roads was 'that devil' Forrest's finest day.

Forrest returned to harassing Sherman's supply line, first clearing East Tennessee of enemy forces. In early November he scared the Federals at Johnsonville into burning vast quantities of supplies and a whole fleet of ships, all of it totaling some $6,700,000 worth of Union property. Despite the success of the Rebel raiders, however, Sherman's advance was inexorable. In November Sherman and his army cut away from their supply lines and set out east across Georgia in their March to the Sea, foraging and burning as they went. Behind them they left Atlanta in ashes. The Union juggernaut had become too much for Forrest or anyone else to stop. In the last days of the war he was made a lieutenant general, but could not halt the Union advance into Alabama; it was his only real loss of the war.

Forrest's later career lacked the glamour of Mosby's. He was associated with the Ku Klux Klan at its formation and became its first Grand Wizard, though he resigned from the organization in 1869. He worked in planting and railroading without regaining his former fortune and died in Memphis in 1877, aged 56. In later years someone asked Confederate General J E Johnston (Sherman's adversary in the Atlanta Campaign) who was the greatest soldier of the war. Without hesitation Johnson named Nathan Bedford Forrest, 'who, had he had the advantages of a thorough military education and training, would have been the great central figure of the Civil War.' Whether or not that is true it was certainly true that, except for Lee's operations, the South was losing on its own territory more often than not throughout the war, and by keeping Forrest in small commands, Jefferson Davis hamstrung the only man who might have been a match for Grant and Sherman. But as with his fellow raiders Morgan and Mosby, Forrest's exploits had an impact far out of proportion to the small number of horsemen he commanded.

The Union Horsemen
Ride to Victory

At the war's beginning the Union command structure was in a state from which it would recover only after three years of rapid command shifts. Guiding Federal operations at the outset was General Winfield Scott, who first saw action in the War of 1812 and was now an aged and debilitated campaigner. Scott had never had much use for cavalry and still did not; echoing an opinion that went back to George Washington, he opined that cavalry was useless in broken or wooded country. Nonetheless, regular-army recruitment went on, mostly in the cities and towns of the North, pulling young Yellowlegs into training camps without worrying too much if they'd ever been acquainted with life on horseback.

In fact, few of the recruits were riders at all, and the camps quickly became scenes of low comedy, as described by one officer who recalled:

The general was sounded, "Boots and Saddles" blown, and Major Falls commanded, "SHOUN! 'AIR T'-A-O-U-N-T!'"
Such a rattling, jingling, jerking, scrambling, cursing I never before heard. Green horses – some of them never had been ridden – turned round and round, backed against each other, jumped up or stood up like trained circus horses. Some of the boys had a pile in front, on their saddles, and one in the rear, so high and heavy it took two men to saddle one horse and two men to help the fellow in his place. The horses sheered out, going sidewise, pushing the well-disposed animals out of position, etc. Some of the boys had never rode anything since they galloped on a hobbyhorse, and clasped their legs close together, thus unconsciously sticking the spurs into their horses' sides . . .

In less than ten minutes the Tenth New York Cavalrymen might have been seen on every hill for two miles rearward. Blankets slipped from under saddles and hung by one corner; saddles slid back until they were on the rumps of the horses; others turned and were on the underside of the animals; horses running and kicking; tin pans, messkettles,

Previous pages: *General George B McClellan and the 5th Cavalry crossing Bull Run at Blackburn's Ford.*

Above: *A Union mule team bogs down and its driver is threatened by a frustrated officer – 'Get that team out of the mud!'*

Below: *Rush's Lancers – the 6th Pennsylvania Cavalry – as depicted by Winslow Homer from a wartime sketch.*

patent sheet-iron camp-stoves, the boys had seen advertised in the illustrated newspapers and sold by the sutlers . . . flying through the air.

These were the recruits with whom the Union Cavalry was about to take on Jeb Stuart.

Aiming for a mounted strength of six regiments, Winfield Scott and his staff reorganized the mounted forces – all of them called cavalry for the first time. The 1st and 2nd Dragoons were now the 1st and 2nd Cavalry, the Mounted Rifles became the 3rd Cavalry, and the old 1st and 2nd Cavalry were renamed the 5th and 6th Cavalry. Hidebound by tradition, Northern generals began the war by ignoring the already-developed breechloading and repeating rifles that, later in the war, would help turn the tide for the Union (and in the process contribute to the obsolescence of mounted soldiers). Thus the Union Cavalry rode to war with sabers strapped under their legs, many of them carrying a muzzle-loading single-shot horse pistol that had a recoil vicious enough to kick the unwary out of the saddle (some men had newer muzzle-loading six-shooters, for which one could carry extra snap-in chambers).

Federal generals' notions of cavalry tactics were equally traditional – just like Frederick the Great's horsemen, the Union Cavalry was primarily intended to function as saber-wielding shock troops. The horseman on the field soon learned, however, that they were more effective in riding to the scene of action and dismounting to shoot – in short, fighting like dragoons.

Another reason Scott downplayed mounted troops was that, since everyone expected a short war, it seemed cavalry was both too expensive and too time-consuming to outfit and train. However, there was a good deal of public pressure for mounted units. Sensitive, as always, to that pressure, President Lincoln authorized any and all volunteers to sign up. This well-intentioned response led to further absurdities. Various men of means assembled their own outfits and received their commissions as officers of volunteers (though some groups elected their officers and, when push came to shove, were apt to find those officers ungrateful and to say so).

The result of all this private initiative was a helter-skelter collection of volunteer outfits sporting such fanciful designations as the Light Horse, Hussars, Dragoons, Mounted Rifles and the like. Many of them were grandly clad, most as green as the hills when it came to fighting. These in turn were ripe prey for crooked horsetraders and outfitters. Contemplating the inevitable chaos, one private wrote, 'The blind led the blind, and often both fell into the same ditch, though not always at the same time.' Not surprisingly, it was to be several years before Federal horsemen were whipped into an effective fighting force.

A Mathew Brady photograph taken at Army of the Potomac headquarters in 1864: Captain Edward A Flint and his mount.

After the Union humiliation at First Bull Run, Lincoln replaced Winfield Scott as commander of Federal Armies with General George B McClellan, a former Dragoon who had studied military science in Europe and brought back his own adaptation of a European military saddle. A lightweight wooden tree covered with rawhide and bristling with hooks and loops for equipment, the McClellan Saddle was made standard issue for Federal Cavalry during the war. McClellan spent only a few months as overall Union commander, but considerably longer as leader of the Union Army of the Potomac, which he built up to be the principal Union Army without being able to lead it to a decisive victory.

McClellan's Army of the Potomac took shape over the end of 1861 and into 1862; it attained a strength of 560 regiments of infantry and 90 of cavalry. Heading the Cavalry Corps was General George Stoneman, 39 years old and, like McClellan, a former Dragoon, veteran of fighting in the West and in Mexico. Described as a figure 'lithe, severe, gristly, sanguine . . . whose eyes flashed even in repose,' Stoneman had been promoted ahead of his old senior officer in the Dragoons, Philip St George Cooke. Cooke probably saw this as the injustice it was, but he was a man who did his duty. One possible reason Cooke was passed over was that he was Virginia-born and all the rest of his family went with the Confederacy – including his daughter, the wife of Jeb Stuart, and his son John, who became a general in Lee's Army. In addition, the rigors of Dragoon life, beginning with the Dodge Expedition, had taken their toll on Cooke's health.

Despite his experience in the Dragoons, General McClellan never used his cavalry as a true fighting unit. Rather, he parceled them out among his other divisions to scout, take messages, guard and often to run errands and police the camp. It was not long before Union infantrymen took up the sardonic and often-repeated gibe, 'Who ever saw a dead cavalryman?'

As mentioned earlier, McClellan and his Army of the Potomac began the Peninsular Campaign in the summer of 1872, moving by ship to the bottom of the peninsula between the York and James Rivers in Virginia and then marching overland toward Richmond. As always, McClellan moved slowly, convinced by his intelligence reports – which came not from his cavalry but from Allan Pinkerton's agents – that he was vastly outnumbered (actual enemy strength was more nearly half his). Exasperated at McClellan's continual demand for reinforcements, Lincoln complained, 'Sending reinforcements to McClellan is like shovelling flies across a barn.' The result of the Peninsular Campaign we have already seen – it accomplished little except to chew up the lives of a great many soldiers. McClellan had not exactly been defeated, but he had been outgeneraled and chased from Virginia. His army was outfought, and Jeb Stuart had ridden circles around him.

After Pope's defeat in the Second Bull Run, McClellan resumed command of the war in the East, still keeping his cavalry subservient and retaining Stoneman as their commander. Although General Pope had given his cavalry their head for a few days before the battle, sending John Buford and others out to raid and scout, the

Above, left: *Union cavalrymen of the 3rd Pennsylvania at Brandy Station, Virginia, scene of the Civil War's greatest cavalry battle.*

Above: *The 7th New York Cavalry encamped near Washington, DC. In the foreground are General I N Palmer and his staff.*

Right: *A Captain of Cavalry, USA, showing saddle equipment and saber.*

first great chapter in the history of Union Cavalry was to be written in the Western theater, during the Vicksburg campaign.

General Ulysses S Grant had made a name for himself with his capture of Forts Henry and Donelson on the Mississippi River. After those campaigns only Vicksburg remained as a stumbling block, and a big one, to Federal control of the river. Through that riverside city funneled arms and supplies from the West into the heart of the Confederacy; to conquer it would choke off a vital lifeline of the South.

Beginning in October of 1862, Grant commenced a series of experiments in approaching Vicksburg that went on for six months. During these operations one of his soldiers grumbled, 'The old fool has tried this . . . five times already, but he's got thirty-seven more plans.' By March 1863, Grant was ready to begin his boldest move yet, one that required precise co-ordination of operations going on all over the maps of Louisiana, Mississippi and into Tennessee. The first major step was to get his army across the river into Mississippi. While he was doing that he needed a diversion of enemy attention, for which task he picked cavalryman Benjamin H Grierson, a former music teacher who had been a soldier for only a year.

Grant gave Colonel Grierson 1000 men and ordered him to start at La Grange, in western Tennessee, and ride south through Mississippi to Union-held Baton Rouge. In the process, Grierson was to make as much noise and cause as much mayhem as possible. Grierson and his Yellowlegs pulled out of La Grange on 17 April 1863. Next day they saw their first action in a

skirmish with local Rebel militia. With his mandate to function as a smokescreen for Grant, Grierson began creating some smokescreens of his own, sending two detachments in different directions to attract enemy forces. The plan worked beautifully: Confederate Cavalry took off after the detachments, mistaking them for Grierson's main column, and Grierson continued into Mississippi virtually unimpeded.

Back in Vicksburg, Confederate commander J C Pemberton swallowed the bait. He was informed that 'Several columns of Federal cavalry starting from different points were making inroads into the northern part of Mississippi and one of them, under Colonel Grierson, was apparently strong enough and bold enough to push on perhaps to the southern limits of the department.' Desperately, Pemberton commandeered some farm horses and installed infantrymen on them, then sent them out to find Grierson. Along with these improvised cavalrymen went all the footsoldiers Pemberton could spare (had he known what Grant was up to, he would have known he had none to spare).

With enemy forces crisscrossing the state trying to find him and his scattered forces, Grierson's main column proceeded South with little resistance, raiding as they went. Rebel detachments finally began closing around the Union column, and a major skirmish developed at Wall's Bridge, near the Louisiana line, where Grierson's men had to drive away three companies of enemy cavalry. Not wanting to press his luck, Grierson rode the last 76 miles to Baton Rouge nonstop in 28 hours.

On 2 May the exhausted and begrimed Federal Cavalrymen rode into Baton Rouge. By then Port Gibson, below Vicksburg, had fallen to the Union and Grant's Army was marching across Mississippi. Grierson and his men had ridden through 600 miles of hostile territory in 16 days, caused 100 enemy casualties, captured over 500 prisoners, wrecked some 60 miles of railroad and telegraph line, destroyed many enemy guns and supplies, and captured 1000 horses and mules. Union losses on the raid were 27 casualties. (Vicksburg was to fall to the Union on 3 July, the same day that Pickett's Charge was being shot to pieces at Gettysburg. The South would never recover from these two disasters.)

Grierson's report to Grant was both astute and encouraging: 'They have neither the arms nor the resources we have given them credit for'; the Confederacy, he said, is 'but a hollow shell, strong on the surface by reason of organized armies, but hollow within, and destitute.' Grant and Sherman would prove the accuracy of that report. Later, Grant wrote of the raid, 'It has been one of the most brilliant cavalry exploits of the war, and will be handed down in history as an example to be imitated.' He could just as well have put it another way: Grierson's raid was worthy of Jeb Stuart himself.

As we saw, Lincoln had made two changes of command in the Army of the Potomac by

Below: *A Brady photograph of Union horseman, Lieutenant Colonel Orson H Hart, taken at Brandy Station, Virginia, in 1864.*

Above: *A battlefield sketch of General Philip Kearny during the Peninsula Campaign of 1862.*

Left: *Federal cavalry generals Pleasanton and Bayard, with Colonel Percy Wyndham in the background, making a reconnaissance near Fredericksburg, Virginia.*

101

January of 1863, finally giving it to General Joseph 'Fighting Joe' Hooker. In contrast to some Union generals who saw that particular post as something to be avoided, Hooker had schemed plenty to get it. Hooker inherited an army that time and again had marched off full of strength and confidence only to be whipped by the Rebels. With unaccustomed vigor he set about the task of revitalizing and reorganizing the Army of the Potomac. Among many changes he vowed to make the cavalry more aggressive. As Union Cavalry officer Wesley Merritt later wrote, 'It was then that we commenced practicing the lessons which the enemy had taught us. From the day of its reorganization under

Hooker, the cavalry of the Army of the Potomac commenced new life.' Hooker consolidated all the mounted units, which had previously been scattered throughout the army, into one Cavalry Corps of 12,000 horsemen under General George Stoneman (by the end of their stay in Washington the army had some 150,000 men in all). Under Stoneman were Generals William W Averell, David M Gregg, John Buford and Alfred Pleasonton.

We have already seen how Hooker carried out his campaign against Lee, and its disastrous conclusion at Chancellorsville. It remains to be seen how carefully Hooker prepared that campaign, which floundered not in the planning but in the execution – and in the fighting spirit of 'Fighting Joe,' which failed him at the critical moment. Hooker's plan was three-pronged: taking most of the cavalry, General Stoneman was to make a Jeb Stuart-style raid around Lee's left, cutting the enemy's communications with Richmond; meanwhile, the rest of the Federal Army would split in two, one small detachment to hold Lee in place at Fredericksburg and the rest to march around and attack his army from the rear.

With 10,000 riders, Stoneman left on 13 April, determined that his men would show their stuff against Jeb Stuart. However, they immediately ran into a foe stronger than Stuart – the weather. Swollen by heavy rains, the Rappahannock River was impassable; it stayed that way for two weeks while the Union horsemen fretted and fumed on its banks. Finally, on 29 April, they forded the river and began their raid.

Stoneman's force, intended as an advance operation, ended up crossing the river on the same day as Hooker's infantry downstream. Curious as to what the Yankee Cavalry might be up to, Stuart galloped over to the crossing, secured some Federal prisoners, found out that Hooker was on the move and then coolly preceeded to ignore Stoneman; he chose instead to shadow the Federal infantry. Thus Hooker moved toward Lee blinded both by his own lack of cavalry and by the enemy's cavalry screen. Against adversaries as dangerous as Lee and Jackson, it was a formula for disaster.

Meanwhile, Stoneman, his command now stripped to about 3500 men, rode south in a cold drenching rain. After tearing up a few railroad tracks, he issued this grandiloquent directive to his commanders: 'I gave them to understand that we had dropped in that region ... like a shell, and that I intended to burst it in every direction, expecting each piece of fragment to do as much harm as the whole shell, and thus magnify our numbers.' In the end, his bombshell proved to be rather a fizzle.

They raided around, wrecked some railroads and burned stores here and there. One contingent, under Judson Kilpatrick, made its way to within two miles of Richmond. While the ladies of Richmond cowered at the sound of cannonfire, a grim-faced Jefferson Davis rode out to inspect his capital's defenses. He needn't have worried. On 4 May Rooney Lee's division routed a column led by Stoneman at Shannon's Crossroads. At Chancellorsville that same day, Lee and Jeb Stuart achieved their historic victory over an army twice their size.

Four days later Stoneman and his men were back with their defeated army. On their raid the Federal Cavalrymen had lost nearly a hundred casualties and some 7000 horses and had harmed the enemy not at all. Certainly, Hooker would have been better off had he kept his cavalry with him; the Union horse might have made the difference at Chancellorsville. But that was not his only mistake in that disastrous month – at the first unexpected brush with Lee's army he

Headquarters of the 13th New York Cavalry at Prospect Hill, Virginia, in July 1865, when military occupation of the South was underway.

had ordered his advance to halt. As he later admitted, 'To tell the truth, I just lost faith in Joe Hooker.'

But then came the Battle of Brandy Station, which, as was seen, gave the Federal Cavalry the impetus it had been waiting for. After that engagement the Federal infantrymen were no longer heard to ask, 'Who ever saw a dead cavalryman?' And in fact, the hard-used Army of the Potomac had not lost faith in themselves; they were only waiting for a commander who would let them show their mettle. Soon both Joe Hooker and George Stoneman would be out, and at Gettysburg the Yankee soldiers would come into their own.

We have seen how in the days before Gettysburg the opposing cavalries fought a running series of engagements that kept Lee blinded as to his enemy's position; how Jeb Stuart left on his raid around the Army of the Potomac and further crippled Lee; how General George G Meade succeeded Hooker as Union commander virtually on the eve of battle; and how the two armies crashed together by accident when a Confederate division came marching toward Gettysburg looking for shoes.

On that day, 1 July 1863, the Confederates were met by John Buford's cavalry at the foot of Seminary Ridge, just west of Gettysburg. At 37, Buford was already an old cavalryman, one of the best the Union had. An acquaintance described his 'quiet dignity, covering a fiery spirit.' That day at Gettysburg was to be his day of glory, and very nearly his epitaph; already suffering from the effects of illness and a severe wound, he was to die of exhaustion and exposure before the year was out.

Buford had hunches about a number of things. Unlike most of his superiors, he had noted the strategic position of Gettysburg, with its many road crossings, and he had expected trouble there. He had a hunch too about the best way for modern cavalrymen to fight: they should ride to the action, dismount and use their rifles – preferably repeating carbines. In those ideas he

was to prove a prophet, and he proved it on that first of July. Strung out in a thin line against vastly superior numbers of enemy infantry, Buford's Yellowlegs peppered away with Spencer repeating carbines and artillery and slowed the enemy advance, giving Union infantry time to move up into position. It was this heroic delaying action by Buford and his cavalrymen that set up the chain of events that would result in the Union position coming to rest on Cemetery Ridge that night, and from there winning the battle. The first shots were fired around ten in the morning; by noon both armies were moving up fast, ready to give it everything they had. It was to be the first time that the two greatest armies of the war, the Union Army of the Potomac and Lee's Army of Northern Virginia, fought a pitched battle at full strength (at Chancellorsville Lee had won without Longstreet's entire division).

We have already examined the rest of the battle from the cavalryman's perspective, including the mounted engagements of 3 July that went on during Pickett's Charge. In the days after his defeat, Lee made his getaway in heavy rains, harried by Union Cavalry. For several days Meade's infantrymen were too exhausted to pursue. On 5 July Judson Kilpatrick struck Lee's rear and took 1000 prisoners. But even after devastating defeat, Lee was wary and dangerous as ever; throwing back all Federal efforts to stop him, he got most of his army safely over the Potomac into Virginia on 13-14 July. The Confederate Army would go on fighting, but in the matter of cavalry and all other aspects, the tide had turned toward the Union.

After the gigantic convulsion of Gettysburg, there was little fight left in the two armies of the East for the rest of 1863 and into 1864. But in February of the latter year, there was an interesting sideshow involving Union Cavalry, which centered in the person of General Judson Kilpatrick. Although he had been promoted to general at the age of 27, Kilpatrick was unpopular with his superiors, one of whom character-

Above: *Union Generals George G Meade, John Sedgwick and Robert O Taylor with staff officers at Horse Artillery headquarters in Virginia. Meade commanded the Army of the Potomac from mid-1863 until the end of the war.*

Opposite: *General Philip Sheridan, at left, with his staff: Colonel James Forsythe, General Wesley Merritt, Thomas C Devin and Major General George A Custer, to whom the Confederate flag of truce was brought after his relentless pursuit of Lee's army in its retreat from Richmond.*

Left: *Union Cavalry scouting.*

ized him as 'a frothy braggart, without brains and not over-stocked with desire to fall on the field'; he added that Kilpatrick achieved 'all his reputation by newspapers and political influence.' (A later commander of his, Sherman, was to observe, 'I know Kilpatrick is a hell of a damned fool, but I want just that sort of man to command my cavalry.') The riders of Kilpatrick's Third Cavalry Division called him 'Kill-cavalry,' both for his recklessness and for his habit of

riding off to missions at breakneck gallop, with the result that his horses were usually half-dead when they arrived at the scene of action. In short, Kilpatrick more or less out-Custered George Custer in his penchant for show and publicity.

In February of 1864, Kilpatrick came up with a scheme extravagant even for him and took it directly to Lincoln. Approved by the President, the plan called for Kilpatrick to essay a raid directly into Richmond, to seize the city if possible by a *coup de main*, to release Federal prisoners held there and distribute amnesty proclamations in the very capital of the enemy. Perhaps the Union generals thought it was crazy enough to work.

Just before midnight on 28 February, Kilpatrick galloped hell-for-leather toward Richmond. With him were 3584 hand-picked cavalrymen, six cannons and a number of wagons. Elsewhere in Virginia George Custer was mounting a diversionary raid. Commanding Kilpatrick's advance party was one-legged Colonel Ulric Dahlgren, son of the Union admiral who invented the Navy's most-used cannon, the Dahlgren gun. At 22, Dahlgren was the youngest officer in the Union Army.

Custer quickly got into the thick of things, charging into Jeb Stuart's artillery camp at Charlottesville. (Custer had earned his own dubious reputation with superiors; contemplating Custer's yards of braid and his velvet uni-

The Federal capture of Baton Rouge, Louisiana, in December 1862 enabled Benjamin Grierson and his riders to make their famous diversionary raid through Mississippi the following spring in support of Grant's attack on Vicksburg. Grierson's report to Grant after the 600-mile ride through enemy territory accurately described the Confederacy as 'but a hollow shell, . . . and destitute.'

form, one of Meade's staff observed, 'This officer is one of the funniest looking human beings you ever saw, and looks like a circus rider gone mad'.) Though the only Rebel casualties reported for his action were '4 skillets, 2 campkettles, 4 water-buckets,' Custer did accomplish something of note that night: he had attacked Jeb Stuart's men at home and gotten himself away in one piece.

Meanwhile, Kilpatrick and Dahlgren had slipped both their columns around Wade Hampton and headed toward Richmond, intending to catch the city in a pincer. Kill-cavalry reached his goal north of Richmond on 1 March, with his men and horses played out, as usual. There, confronted with the defenses of the Confederate capital, he apparently thought better of the whole affair; the enemy fortifications were strong and resistance was stiff (one wonders what he expected). He then pulled back, leaving Dahlgren to his fate. That was not long in coming.

Dahlgren had made his way haltingly toward the city, losing troops as he went. Failing to find a river crossing to which he had been directed by a slave, Dahlgren had the man hanged with his own bridle. By the end of 1 March, his column had thrashed its way to within three miles of Richmond, where they were met by enemy forces that claimed more of the dwindling Union detachment. In heavy rain in the middle of the night, Dahlgren and his 100 remaining men retreated north to try to find Kilpatrick. Growing numbers of Rebel cavalry accumulated around him. The whole misbe-

gotten expedition found its inevitable climax on 2 March, when Dahlgren's column was ambushed; most of his men were captured and Dahlgren was shot dead. On his body a 13-year-old boy discovered papers stating that 'The city must be destroyed and Jeff Davis and his cabinet killed.' Needless to say, the entire Confederacy erupted in fury at this planned atrocity, and Lee sent a copy of the papers to Meade with a demand for explanation. Despite all efforts, there was never a satisfactory explanation from anyone – certainly it is unlikely Lincoln would have countenanced such a barbarity, and indeed it was never determined if the papers were authentic (if they were, then Dahlgren had misspelled his own name on them). Safely back in camp, Judson Kilpatrick was content simply to blame Dahlgren for the failure of the whole expedition.

Four days after the Kilpatrick-Dahlgren raid spluttered to its inglorious end, a historic meeting took place at a Washington reception. President Lincoln strode uncertainly up to a short, rather disheveled-looking soldier and queried, 'This is General Grant, is it?' 'Yes,' Grant replied nervously. They had never met before, but Lincoln had just appointed the general to head the entire Union war effort. It was a terrifying responsibility, but in short order Grant had produced the Union's first overall plan to win the war. Typically for his operations, it involved a multi-pronged offensive spread out over the whole country. Only two of those prongs – Sherman's and the one Grant led in person – were to make any headway, but in the end that proved to be enough.

Above: *Troop K of the 10th US Cavalry on the battlefield at Chickamauga, Georgia, in September of 1863. President Lincoln's brother-in-law, Confederate General Ben Hardin Helm, was killed in action here.*

Left: *Union Colonel Ulric Dahlgren, who served under Meade at Gettysburg and lost his life in an abortive raid on Richmond with the reckless Judson Kilpatrick.*

At the Battle of Chattanooga (24–5 November 1863), the Union stormed Lookout Mountain and captured Missionary Ridge. Later, a Union soldier recalled that the presence of General Sherman, 'our beloved commander,' inspired confidence by his 'sharing the danger we were about to undertake.'

Opposite, top: Custer's division retiring from Mount Jackson, during the Valley Campaign of October 1864.

Opposite, bottom: Skilled blacksmiths like this one seen working near Petersburg were in great demand by the armies of both sides.

For his cavalry chief, Grant told Lincoln he wanted 'the very best man in the army.' That man turned out to be a bandy-legged little Irishman named Phil Sheridan, who had begun his military life as an unusually mediocre student at West Point and entered the war as a desk-bound lieutenant. But as soon as Sheridan had gotten into the field he had started winning, and along with Sherman he had been with Grant during the victorious Chattanooga campaign of late 1863. Sheridan was one of the most aggressive generals of the war, but in contrast to the mild manners of both Grant and Lee, 'Little Phil' played the part, being fierce, abrasive and spectacularly foul-mouthed. In battle he took on an almost insane ferocity, though always remaining firmly in control of himself and the situation.

Grant left Meade nominally in charge of the Army of the Potomac, but made his headquarters with that army; clearly, he was determined to direct the destruction of Lee's forces personally. Sheridan succeeded Stoneman as cavalry commander, vowing to make the Yellowlegs a fighting force equal to the infantry. 'I'm going to take the cavalry away from the bobtailed brigadier generals,' he declared. 'They must do without their escorts. I intend to make the cavalry an arm of the service.' That also meant fighting on foot, as John Buford had seen. Sheridan quickly made his presence felt among his men. They learned that if they did their jobs, he would treat them very well indeed – he was more attentive to food supplies than most generals – and if not, they were likely to be shipped out someplace where life was tougher.

At the end of April Grant wrote, 'The Army of the Potomac is in splendid condition and evidently feels like whipping somebody.' On 4 May the army crossed the Potomac and headed into Virginia once more, but this time everyone on both sides seemed to understand that this was the fight to the finish. The first round came quickly, and it was a most bloody and indecisive one. On 5 May Lee jumped Grant's army in the Wilderness of Virginia, near Chancellorsville. In two days of ghastly fighting the Army of the Potomac was barely able to hold its own. Then Grant slipped his army around Lee's right flank and marched toward Richmond. Jeb Stuart reported the movement to Lee, who discerned that the Federals were heading for a road crossing at Spotsylvania. If the Yankees got there first, they would be between Lee and the Confederate capital. Lee determined to beat them, and something of a footrace developed.

The fact that Lee won the race and was waiting for the Union advance when it arrived at Spotsylvania set off a shouting match between Meade and Sheridan. Meade blamed the cavalry for obstructing his infantry on the march; Sheridan replied heatedly that Meade had been trying to command them and caused the problem himself. The upshot was that Meade went off to complain to Grant, telling him that Sheridan had boasted his cavalry could whip Jeb Stuart. Unconcerned with the quarrel, Grant went to the heart of the matter: 'Did Sheridan say that? Well, he generally knows what he is talking about. Let him start right out and do it.'

On 9 May Sheridan and 10,000 cavalrymen pulled away, at a walk, in the general direction of Richmond. Sheridan knew that Jeb Stuart would have to follow him. Soon Stuart obliged, raiding in the Federal rear and then swinging around to get between the enemy and Richmond. Finally, Stuart decided to halt his 8000 men and wait for Sheridan at an abandoned building called Yellow Tavern, six miles from Richmond. On 11

May the Federals arrived before noon and mounted a few probing attacks. Then in late afternoon George Custer rode out, his band playing 'Yankee Doodle,' to lead an assault on Stuart's left flank.

Custer's riders moved toward the enemy at a walk, then increased gait to a trot, then galloped forward at full speed. The Confederate line erupted in fire; the whole battlefield seemed to disappear in smoke. Within a few minutes a mounted countercharge of Virginia cavalry had pushed the Yankees back. In a series of charges and countercharges, the battle roared back and forth past a Confederate officer who sat calmly on his horse directing his men and firing over their heads with his pistol.

Union Private J A Huff was retreating on foot when he noticed that Confederate officer some 15 yards away. Private Huff turned to take a pistol shot at the mounted man. He saw the officer reel in the saddle. It is not recorded if Huff realized he had just bagged Jeb Stuart. The Cavalier was carried from the field writhing in pain, a bullet in his stomach; as he left he raised

himself to gasp, 'Go back! Go back! I had rather die than be whipped.' After a day of agony, he died at the home of his brother-in-law. Perhaps Jeb Stuart would have wanted it that way, to die from a battle wound and not have to watch his cause go down to defeat. For with his passing the power of the Southern Cavalry ended, and along with it another irreplaceable component of Lee's record of victory. Now it was the hard-fighting Sheridan and the Union riders who would write the glorious chapters.

Their leader gone, the Rebel Cavalry pulled back from Yellow Tavern, leaving the road to Richmond open. But Sheridan had no intention of taking on the city; he had gained a big enough prize already. After further raiding and skirmishing, Sheridan rejoined Grant on 24 May. Despite having just fought another bloody and indecisive battle at Spotsylvania, Grant greeted Sheridan cheerfully: it had been a successful raid indeed. With Sheridan's cavalry guarding his flanks, Grant slipped around Lee toward Richmond for the third time. In a few days Custer and Gregg were tangling with Rebel Cavalry under Fitz Lee. In driving the Yankees away, the Confederates proved they were capable of fighting without Jeb Stuart.

On 1 June the Army of the Potomac found itself under attack at Cold Harbor. These attacks were thrown back, partly by Sheridan's men using Spencer repeating rifles (of which a Rebel prisoner had said, 'You-all must sit up all night loadin' them new guns of yourn'). The next day saw an all-out battle at Cold Harbor, in which Grant threw a series of assaults against heavily entrenched Confederate lines that resulted in 7000 Federal casualties to the South's 1500. It was a horrible failure of judgment on the part of Grant, the bitter climax of a month in which he had incurred 50,000 casualties trying to bludgeon Lee into submission. He had failed in that, but knew perfectly well that in the long run the Southern losses, unlike his own, could not be replaced. Unable to whip Lee in the field, he was forced to bleed him to death one drop at a time.

After Cold Harbor, however, Grant changed his strategy of hammering Lee, deciding to pick up his army as quietly as possible and move south to take Petersburg, which was, in effect, the back door to Richmond. Preparing for that move, Grant sent Sheridan on a diversionary raid toward Charlottesville. Lee took the bait, sending Fitz Lee and Wade Hampton, the latter now Stuart's successor as cavalry commander, to

In the trenches at Petersburg, where Lee's hungry men made a last stand against Federal forces. Sheridan cut Lee's last supply lines when he occupied Dinwiddie Court House, forcing the Confederates to retreat and leave Richmond open to the enemy.

stop Sheridan. The forces of Hampton and Sheridan tangled near Trevilian Station. On the Union side the engagement was mishandled from the outset; at one point, Custer was assaulting Hampton's rear when he discovered Fitz Lee on *his* rear – with his customary thoughtless boldness, Custer had ridden right between two enemy columns. It took much of the day for reinforcements to cut their way through to extricate Custer and his men. In a Federal prisoner's diary we find a succinct summary of the progress of the battle: 'June 11. Fight at Trevilian Station. Captured and killed 600 rebs ... June 12th. Fought on same ground. Got whipped like the devil. Lost more men than the rebs did the day previous ... June 13th. Retreat back towards Fredericksburg.' Meanwhile, Lee had figured out what Grant was up to.

Sheridan arrived on 21 June at Petersburg, where Grant's attempts to storm the city had failed and the Army of the Potomac had settled into a siege. Inside the city were Lee and the Army of Northern Virginia. Grant began sending cavalry out to raid the Confederate rail lines, trying to choke off their supplies; in that effort they made little progress. At the end of June, Grant received disturbing news: Confederate General Jubal Early was raiding in Virginia's Shenandoah Valley and heading for Washington. While Grant was not overly worried about the capital (Early actually made it to the defenses of Washington before pulling back), he was concerned about Early tying up troops needed for the Petersburg siege. Finally, as Early continued operations in the Shenandoah into August, Grant ordered Sheridan to do something about it.

For the operation Sheridan was to relinquish control of the Cavalry Corps and assume command of a mixed army of 48,000 infantry, cavalry and artillery. He was to drive Early out of the

Shenandoah, but he was not to stop at that. The fertile valley 100 miles long and some 30 miles wide, was the breadbasket of the Confederacy, its farms providing sustenance for the South's soldiers. The Shenandoah Valley was also the domain of Confederate partisan raider John Mosby and his men. Union control there must eventually starve the Confederacy into submission. Now, as Sherman was already doing in Georgia, the burden of the conflict would fall on the civilians of the South. In the twentieth century, the strategy of waging war on a whole population would be called Total War: Sherman and Sheridan were its harbingers.

Sheridan moved his forces to Harper's Ferry, the northern door of the valley, and began marching south, burning crops and barns and rounding up livestock as he went. Sheridan's depredations fell most heavily upon the area popularly known as Mosby's Confederacy, where locals fed and housed the Rebel raiders.

Below: *Petersburg, Virginia, the gateway to Richmond. After Confederate troops broke out of the city, Sheridan's cavalry intercepted their attempted rendezvous at Amelia Court House.*

Above: *An A R Waud sketch of the Union mine assault at Petersburg, where a three-month siege finally dislodged Confederate defenders.*

For a time Jubal Early waited, letting Sheridan and his army march a third of the way up the valley; then the Yankees headed back, continuing to destroy crops and commandeer livestock. Finally, at the beginning of September Grant sent Sheridan back up the valley with firm orders to engage Early. When he heard from a female spy that Early was closing in, Sheridan made ready to attack. Meanwhile Early, misled by Sheridan's lack of aggressiveness so far, jumped to a most inappropriate conclusion: in Early's own words, 'The events of the last month had satisfied me that the commander opposed to me was without enterprise, and possessed an excessive caution which amounted to timidity.' On 19 September, Sheridan, the least timid of commanders, located Early and struck hard –

General Benjamin Franklin Butler spent $12,000 of his own money on 12 newly invented Gatling mechanical machine guns and ammunition for the siege of Petersburg. In proving out the deadly new weapon, he unwittingly hastened the eventual replacement of the horse by mechanized armored transport.

and then very nearly got himself whipped. Unused to commanding a large mixed force, Sheridan moved his divisions too slowly to swamp the wily old Early. But superior Federal numbers finally prevailed and Early retreated south, hastened by troopers who charged the Rebels with pistols and sabers.

Three days later Sheridan caught up with Early again at Fishers Hill, where the Confederates had taken a strong defensive position. There a subordinate and friend of Sheridan's named George Crook hit Early's flank, as another detachment attacked in front. Sheridan seemed to be riding at every part of the line at once, shouting 'Go on, don't stop, go on!' Finally, seeing the Confederates were breaking, he bellowed 'Forward everything!' Early was routed again, but got away intact. Sheridan turned and headed north again, destroying as he went.

Twice beaten, Early was not giving up. He began collecting men and supplies for another offensive; his artillerymen discovered that a shipment of field guns had been labelled 'For General Sheridan, care of General Early.' The Confederates began to harass Sheridan, who was getting testy about the whole business. Sheridan dismissed one of his generals for lack of aggressiveness and, furious at Early's harassments, ordered General Torbert to 'Whip the enemy or be whipped yourself.' At Tom's Brook on 9 October, Torbert did as ordered. In a spirited two-hour cavalry battle, the participants went from carbines to pistols to sabers before the Confederate divisions were routed, some of them fleeing 20 miles with Federals in hot pursuit (the Yankee riders dubbed the fight 'the Woodstock Races').

No doubt Sheridan then figured he had finished Early once and for all and could take the time to go up to Washington for consultations. He left for Washington on 16 October; by the evening of the 18th he was back in Winchester ready to rejoin his army next day at Cedar Creek, near Middletown. In the morning, as Sheridan made ready to ride back to camp, he heard sporadic firing in the distance. Not particularly worried about it, he mounted his charger Rienzi and headed toward Middletown. When he was about 14 miles from Cedar Creek the sounds of battle grew louder. Sheridan dismounted and put his ear to the ground (throughout the war, sound was one of the most important sources of information – an experienced soldier could hear trouble, hear victory, hear defeat). Puzzled at what he was hearing that morning, Sheridan remounted and rode a little faster.

The Battle of Gettysburg, Pennsylvania: the first day.

Then, coming over a crest, Sheridan saw his army streaming toward him in full retreat, with the usual chaos of men, wagons, mules and horses. Soon he got the report – Early had made a surprise attack on the Federal camp at Cedar Creek just before dawn and sent them running. Spurring Rienzi into a gallop, Sheridan sped forward, waving his strange little hat, and made a charge of his own into his army, turning them around, sending them back toward the enemy. Later, Sheridan was to record that he had said to his men, 'If I had been with you this morning, this disaster would not have happened. We must face the other way; we will go back and recover our camp.' More likely, he simply cussed them back into battle. After Sheridan rode by, one weary officer told his men, 'We may as well do it now; Sheridan will get it out of us some time.'

This was the stuff of legend, and indeed the most famous poem of the war was 'Sheridan's Ride.' And certainly, it was the presence of Sheridan, waving his hat and galloping about, that reversed the Union rout at Cedar Creek. In fact, the Federals had already been mounting resistance before Sheridan arrived – his men were old soldiers by now – and the process of organizing a full counterattack took over five hours of painstaking work. But finally, in late afternoon, Sheridan led his infantry and cavalry, all of them screaming like devils, to the charge.

Sheridan rode forward with them, exulting 'We've got the goddamdest twist on them you ever saw!'

A Confederate officer, his heart sinking after a vision of certain victory, watched the Yankees approach: 'There came from the north side of the plain, a dull heavy swelling sound like a roaring of a distant cyclone, the omen of additional disaster. It was unmistakable. Sheridan's horsemen [it was Custer and his division] riding furiously across the open fields of grass to intercept the Confederates before they crossed.... The only possibility of saving the rear regiments was in unrestrained flight – every man for himself.'

Early's Confederates turned and ran back through the enemy camps they had previously captured. Thus ended the last real offensive the Confederacy was able to mount in the Shenandoah Valley. In February of 1865, Sheridan annihilated Early's last remaining force at Waynesboro. Then he rode back to join Grant in the siege lines of Petersburg. As we have seen, Confederate raider Mosby was never brought to bay, but to discourage civilian co-operation with him, Sheridan sent his men around the valley to gather and burn every speck of food and every bit of fodder. With a vengeance, he had achieved his stated goal: to clean the Shenandoah of food so completely that a crow flying over it would have to carry his own provisions.

Below: *Robert E Lee, commander-in-chief of Confederate armies, was a highly valued US Army officer before his home state of Virginia seceded and he resigned his commission.*

Below right: *Sherman's soldiers receiving their pay in Atlanta before the March to the Sea.*

Sheridan and his army returned to cheers from the weary Army of the Potomac, who were still besieging Petersburg. Resuming command of the cavalry, Sheridan proposed to Grant that the Yellowlegs ride around the city, cutting Lee's supply lines. Grant was dubious, but Lincoln arrived and personally approved the plan. To give him a free hand, Sheridan was made commander-in-chief of the Army of the Shenandoah, which included 12,000 cavalrymen (many with repeating carbines) and two corps of infantry. In heavy rain, Sheridan and his men occupied Dinwiddie Court House, between the two railroad lines that were the lifeline of Lee's army. The Rebels took to calling Little Phil 'Sheridan the Inevitable'; wherever they went or wanted to go, there Sheridan seemed to be.

On 1 April Sheridan attacked and defeated Pickett at Five Forks. During the battle Sheridan rode across the front waving a guidon and shouting his men on (he also cashiered one of his generals on the spot for being too slow). After the engagement, Sheridan went about apologizing to the officers he had insulted. It was this battle that made Lee's position in Petersburg untenable; now the once-victorious general and his starving Army of Northern Virginia had to run, and in the process they must leave Richmond to the enemy.

Before dawn on 2 April, Union assaults began breaking through Lee's lines in Petersburg. The Confederates bolted, heading west in two wings. As a last, desperate hope, Lee was trying to rendezvous with Southern forces in South Carolina. Grant and Sheridan learned that the enemy wings were to join at Amelia Court House, where some rations were being shipped by train. Sherman pulled out to intercept the retreat and swamped one of the wings. Now Lee had lost half of what little army he had left. Time was running out fast for the Confederacy; like an avenging angel, Sheridan the Inevitable seemed to be sweeping closer and closer.

It ended at Appomattox on 9 April. There Sheridan's men pounced on the four trains of rations meant for Lee. Surrounded on all sides, Lee ordered one more charge. For a moment his men broke through Sheridan's cavalry, but the gap was immediately plugged by a sea of Blue infantry. It was over.

The war had begun with shows of pageantry and dreams of gallantry and glory. In the end, it was won for the Union by force of numbers, by professionalism and by sheer bulldog tenacity. As often happens in war, the early losers in the game learned their lessons from the victors and turned their own tactics against them to win. That in essence was the story of the Union Cavalry in the Civil War – though a vital part of the formula too was the fighting spirit of Phil Sheridan and his magical ability to infuse that spirit into the whole Union Cavalry.

Top left: *Jefferson Davis, President of the Confederacy, was charged with treason after the war but never tried. After his release from prison, he retired to Beauvoir, an estate on the Gulf of Mexico, and wrote his memoirs of the war.*

Above: *The grand review of Union troops in Washington, DC, at the close of the Civil War.*

117

Right: *Sheridan rallies his troops at Winchester.*

Opposite, top: *The Battle at Five Forks, Virginia.*

Opposite, bottom: *Union commanders survey the scene of the Battle of Chattanooga.*

Above: *A Reader painting of Union horsemen preparing to go into battle.*

Right: *Sixth Union Cavalry charge at Brandy Station – 11 October 1863.*

The Great Indian Wars in the West

Previous pages: A Dash for the Timber on the frontier, vividly depicted by Frederic Remington.

Below: The infamous Sand Creek massacre of peaceful Cheyenne and Arapaho villagers in what is now Colorado, led by Indian-hating Colonel John M Chivington. Both the American flag and a flag of truce flew over the lodge of chief Black Kettle when the attack began.

Opposite, top: A US Cavalry bugler is felled by hostile Indians in this Schreyvogel painting titled Surrounded.

Opposite, bottom: Frederic Remington's Dismounted: The 4th Troopers Moving *epitomizes the energy and excitement of the artist's best work.*

The history of the US Cavalry after the Civil War is the history of the final conquest and subjugation of America's native population. It is a story as heroic and exciting as any, but despite the vainglorious image of this era in movies and books, it is an inescapably tragic story as well.

When the white man arrived, the Indians owned their own land by natural right. Thus justice was ultimately on the side of the Indians in the ensuing conflict. But history was on the side of the whites. In the years after the Civil War, the waves of settlers pushing West swelled to a flood that would never abate. In their push to settle the land from coast to coast, the settlers considered it their right to displace the natives more or less at will. The only official restraint on this assumption was the need to make some appearance, at least, of fairness and legality. In the long run, however, the whites were clearly determined to take whatever land they wanted by whatever means necessary.

From the time Columbus arrived and branded the native people with the absurd name of Indians – believing himself to be in the West Indies – the clash of white and Indian cultures was a morass of ignorance and misunderstanding. What everyone on both sides did understand, however, the thing that all men have understood at all times, was *power*. And in that sphere the Indians possessed a few advantages: some of the Indian cultures, most notably the Sioux, Cheyenne and Apache, were unsurpassed fighters. One on one, they could outfight any white man, and they were fighting on and for their own territory. But just as the Indians' culture and habits of thought made it impossible for them to understand whites, so Indian culture made it very difficult for them to fight concerted campaigns. Indian societies were usually democratic, decisions being made by the consensus of chiefs; thus their military operations lacked a central command and a large-scale strategy. Beyond that, ancient tribal rivalries made alliances strained and tenuous. Sooner or later, even the alliances forged by great leaders like Crazy Horse fell apart, and such alliances were the exception rather than the rule. All successful opponents of the Indians understood this fact and made use of tribal rivalries for their own purposes. Since power rather than justice ruled, the resistance of the Indians was doomed from the beginning by the white man's superior strategic skills, as well as by the sheer number of settlers and their incurable lust for land.

What is remarkable is that Indian resistance lasted as long as it did. A major factor in this was that the Indians, besides being great fighters, had a remarkable ability to make the white man fight on their terms and in their style, which was hit-and-run guerrilla warfare – the despair of organized armies from the time of the Mongols to the war in Vietnam.

White authorities, even sympathetic ones, could only envision one end for the Indians: these peoples of a proud and ancient hunting and fighting tradition were either to be killed or to be herded onto reservations to exist on government handouts until they could be forcibly converted into farmers. The Indians, in short, had to be broken in will and spirit and transformed into small dirt farmers and decent Christians. The fact that this would erase native cultures and religions seemed to most whites to be a positive virtue of the policy. Bewildered, often betrayed, prey to the usually corrupt and indifferent Indian Bureau and to crooked traders and bootleggers, crushed by forces beyond their experience and comprehension, it was for the Indians as if their universe had fallen down on top of them.

Thus a realistic account of this era will not often resemble the exhilarating Hollywood image of the hell-for-leather cavalryman. For the Yellowlegs it was a hard, dangerous and bloody job they were called on to do, much of it dirty work indeed. Yet it had its moments of glory, remarkable feats of heroism on both sides, and now and then even episodes of real under-standing, of humanity and justice. In any case, for the horse cavalry it was to be their most difficult and all-but-final, challenge.

At 1:30 AM on 27 November 1868, the Cheyenne village of Chief Black Kettle slept

along the banks of the Washita River (in what is now Oklahoma). Black Kettle had long been a peace advocate and a pacifying element among his people, but this had not prevented him from being attacked by Chivington in 1864. No matter which Indians went on the warpath, soldiers and settlers were likely to strike back at any Indians handy. This was about to happen to Black Kettle and his people again, and for the last time. A squaw saw soldiers coming and screamed a warning. In another moment a column of US Cavalry roared into the village, pistols blazing, the company band playing away on freezing instruments. Black Kettle, emerging from his tepee, was riddled with bullets. Within a half hour 103 warriors were cut down, 53 women and children taken prisoner. The attacking cavalrymen lost 22 killed and 14 wounded. As was their custom, the Cheyenne warriors mutilated the corpses of their enemies, but before long most of the warriors were dead too, many of them scalped by the cavalrymen. Among the dead were several white captives who had been killed by Indian women when the attack began. All around lay the dead, freezing quickly in the winter cold. It was a successful raid for the 7th United States Cavalry. Its

commander, General George Armstrong Custer, was in his element.

Custer's raid was part of a large offensive against the Cheyenne and Arapaho in Kansas and Colorado, where an uprising by those tribes in 1868 had claimed the lives of 117 settlers. Seasoned cavalryman Philip Sheridan was in command of the area. He had taken the offensive after prodding from his superior in Washington, General of the Army William T Sherman, who had said of the Indian offensive: 'The more we can kill this year, the less we'll have to kill next year, for the more I see of these Indians the more I am convinced that they all have to be killed or be maintained as a species of paupers.' This was to prove a succinct summary of the whole progress of the Indian wars. As for Sheridan, the man in charge of operations against the Plains tribes, he was said to have originated the phrase 'The only good Indian is a dead Indian.' After Custer's attack on the Washita, Sheridan considered the Indians in the area properly subdued.

This was the beginning of the final push against the Indians of the West, although it took over 20 more years to subdue the last of the uprisings. Operations in the West had naturally slackened during the Civil War, and Indian power and confidence had grown accordingly in the absence of strong resistance. Still, there was plenty of action and fighting in the West during the war. One non-cavalry endeavor was to become part of American legend despite its short history – the Pony Express, a fast mail service between St Joseph, Missouri, and Sacramento, California, that lasted from April 1860 to the end of 1861. Using chains of horses

ATTENTION! INDIAN
FIGHTERS

Having been authorized by the Governor to raise a Company of 100 day

U. S. VOL CAVALRY!

For immediate service against hostile Indians. I call upon all who wish to engage in such service to call at my office and enroll their names immediately.

Pay and Rations the same as other U. S. Volunteer Cavalry.

Parties furnishing their own horses will receive 40c per day, and rations for the same, while in the service.

The Company will also be entitled to all horses and other plunder taken from the Indians.

Office first door East of Recorder's Office.

HAL SAYR.

Central City, Aug. 13, '64.

and riders stationed in 190 posts, the Express carried the mail an astonishing 250 miles a day. During its short history it was remarkably free from interference by Indians, not to mention from fierce winter weather and wild animals. Among the young riders were men like 'Buffalo Bill' Cody and 'Wild Bill' Hickok. For all the glory and attention the Pony Express has received, however, the service was soon doomed by the coming of the transcontinental telegraph in October 1861.

Another figure of Western legend was fighting in the West during the war years – scout Kit Carson, who led operations against his old friends the Navajos and imposed a bitter relocation on them (though later they were returned to their old area). Also during the Civil War, General H H Sibley tore the Sioux out of their hunting grounds and drove them to the Southwest; it was the beginning of 30 years of war against that proud warrior tribe. In November 1867, cavalrymen in what is now Colorado, led by a fanatical Indian-hating colonel named John M Chivington, pounced on Black Kettle's peaceful village of Cheyenne and Arapaho and massacred 500 of its residents, mostly women and children. Indian fighter Nelson A Miles was later to call the Chivington massacre 'perhaps the foulest and most unjustifiable crime in the annals of America.' It was also very unwise, as it made those tribes among the most resentful and implacable Indian raiders in the country, with decades of suffering and death as a result. Meanwhile, during the war the wagon trains of settlers continued to move into the West. By 1870 there were more whites in Kansas alone than there were Indians in the entire United States.

After the Civil War the US Army faced divided responsibilities with declining numbers of troops. They had to occupy the South, patrol the Mexican border and deal with the Indians. The experienced cavalrymen who wanted to remain in the service gradually moved on to life in the Western outposts, which were scattered around Indian Territory and on the Mexican border. New recruits began coming in, but they were an unpromising lot. Many were immigrants, most had little schooling and, not infrequently, criminal records as well. However drunken and unruly the new Yellowlegs proved on the post, though, they usually did the job in the field.

Top: *Black Kettle's people were attacked again along the Washita River in 1868; this time, the Cheyenne leader lost his life. The 7th Cavalry under George Custer made the raid in reprisal for unrelated uprisings in Kansas and Colorado.*

Above: *US Cavalry troopers at ease in their camp at the base of Gillem's Bluff during the Modoc Wars.*

Right: *Cavalry Lieutenant S C Robertson, Chief of the Crow Scouts.*

Above: *The massacre of five settlers in Meeker County, Minnesota, by Eastern Sioux or Santees (17 August 1862) touched off an Indian war that resulted in hundreds of deaths on both sides.*

Left: *The black 10th Cavalry regiment, commanded by white officers, fought in the Geronimo campaign in 1886; depicted here,* The Rescue of Corporal Scott, *by Remington.*

Left: *A US Cavalry column crossing a ford in the last year of the Indian Wars, by Rufus Zogbaum.*

Above: *The short-lived Pony Express mail service between St Joseph, Missouri, and Sacramento, California, galloped into American legend in the early 1860s.*

Top: Dead Sure *by Charles Schreyvogel shows troopers armed with the Colt .45 single-action revolver (1873).*

Life on the posts varied in comfort, but was rarely less than difficult. The cavalryman's day was regulated by the post bugler, who sounded Assembly, Recall, Reveille, Mess, Taps, and the many other calls in the repertoire. Summer was filled with mounted and dismounted drill, horse grooming, stable cleaning, inspection, guard duty and the thousand similar chores of military life. A morass of tradition and protocol ruled the procedures of the forts; for example, the old tradition that a new commanding officer could select his own quarters often created a ludicrous shuffling all the way down the chain of command, since everyone lower down got to pick new quarters as well.

Officers' quarters on the posts varied from grim and primitive to spacious and elegant houses like the one in which George and Libby Custer came to rest at Fort Lincoln. The wives faced their own challenges, besides the incessant fear for their husbands' lives. Food supplies often had to come from enormous distances, and women learned to cook without staples like eggs and milk. Children were taught at home before being shipped East to complete their education. In their leisure time, the troops relaxed mainly in the traditional ways – with liquor, gambling and prostitutes. In winter, when there were few duties, boredom became epidemic for the enlisted men, while the officers partied and socialized at an endless series of balls.

On the trail, the horse soldiers scarcely resembled their later Hollywood counterparts. Many wore issue trousers patched with canvas, coats of various issue from the Civil War on, and white or grey felt civilian hats rather than the uniform black campaign hat. George Custer and a few other officers affected fringed buckskins. After 1873 troopers carried that year's Springfield repeating carbine slung on a strap around the body, and a model 1872 Colt six-shooter. Some sported homemade cartridge belts. Sabers were rarely seen.

Four new mounted divisions were created in 1866, when Congress established the 7th through 10th Cavalries. The 9th and 10th consisted of black troopers with white officers. These two outfits were to see as much action as their white counterparts over the coming decades, though they suffered from the racist attitudes that remained endemic in the US Army after the war. Their fighting record was distinguished; indeed, the caliber of black troopers was generally higher than white, since military service represented a rare opportunity for ambitious blacks, while it was often a repository for the dregs of white society. The black cavalrymen came to be called 'Buffalo Troopers,' the name reportedly originating with Indians who first saw the blacks in buffalo robes and thought their hair was also contrived from the

buffalo's hide. The early operations of the Buffalo Troopers were mainly in Kansas and Texas, but later they fought all over the map, earning a number of Medals of Honor in the process. The 9th Cavalry saved the 7th in the aftermath of Wounded Knee, and black troopers fought beside Roosevelt at San Juan Hill.

The cavalry horse Comanche, sole survivor of the battle at the Little Big Horn.

Opposite, top: General Custer (in fringed buckskins) at Fort Abraham Lincoln, Dakota Territory, with staff members and their families.

Opposite, bottom: A scout with the Buffalo Soldiers, as sketched by Remington at Sierra Bonitos in 1888.

Right: The Last of the Redskins, an engraving by Gautier, depicts the Indian as noble savage. Many 19th-century Americans were deeply disturbed by the injustices perpetrated against the country's original inhabitants.

As for the Indians, they led their traditional lives as best they could. Many of them were already on reservations by the end of the war. Among the most aggressive of the Plains tribes were the Sioux and Cheyenne in the north, both peoples being superb horsemen. (The Indians, of course, had not had horses until the Spanish and other Europeans brought them to the New World.) Of the Comanches, to the south, an observer wrote, 'Every warrior has a war horse, which is the fleetest that can be obtained, and he prizes him more highly than anything else in his possession.' Painter George Catlin described the horsemanship of the Comanche warrior, who could ride hanging over the side of the animal with one foot hooked over its back: 'In this wonderful position he will hang whilst his horse is at the fullest speed, carrying with him his bow and shield, and also his long lance ... all or either of which he will wield upon his enemy as he passes; riding and throwing his arrows over the horse's back or under the horse's neck.'

All Indians fought as guerrillas, picking their own place and time to engage the enemy. An associate of General George Crook wrote, 'The Apache was in no sense a coward. He knew his business and played his cards to suit himself. He never lost a shot or lost a warrior when a brisk run across the nearest ridge would save a life or exhaust the heavily-clad soldier who endeavored to catch him.' While the Apaches traditionally stole their horses, the Comanches maintained herds sometimes several times larger than the number of people in the tribe.

The Sioux warrior, General George Crook said, 'is a cavalry soldier from the time he has intelligence enough to ride a horse, [and] they can move at the rate of 50 miles a day.' Throughout the Indian wars, those who esteemed the Indians' fighting abilities most were their Army opponents: one of Crook's officers called the Plains Indians 'the finest light cavalry in the world.'

Philip Sheridan took command of the Department of Missouri in 1868, a year before completion of the Union Pacific Railroad prepared the way for thousands more settlers to move in – and for the hunters who would devastate the buffalo herds that were the life of many Indian tribes. Sheridan oversaw military operations across 150,000 square miles of Kansas, Colorado, New Mexico and Indian Territory. For that purpose he had, absurdly enough, only 1200 cavalrymen and 1400 infantry, stationed in 26 forts. Despite the size of his forces, the pugnacious Sheridan immediately took the offensive. Naturally, his initial tactics were derived from his Civil War experience: thus he would send out large bodies of men in an effort to surround hostile tribes. Occasionally, as with Custer's devastation of Black Kettle's village, these tactics worked. But in the field it was finally realized that what worked better were tactics based on Indian style – small, quick and mobile actions stressing hit-and-run raids. Most of the time the cavalrymen rode to the action and then fought dismounted, every fourth man holding the horses.

The kind of depredations the Yellowlegs were expected to stop can be seen in three days of Sheridan's record for 1868:

September 1st, near Lake Station ... a woman and child killed and scalped and thirty head of stock run off by Indians; at Reed's Springs, three persons were killed and three wounded; at Spanish Fort, Texas, four persons were murdered, eight scalped, fifteen horses and mules run off and three women outraged; one of these women was outraged by thirteen Indians who afterwards killed and scalped her and then killed her four little children.

September 2nd, on Little Coon Creek, Kansas, a wagon ... attacked by about forty Indians. Three of the [cavalry escort] were badly wounded; three Indians were killed and one wounded.

September 4th, Major Tilford, 7th Cavalry, Commanding Fort Reynolds, Colorado, reported four persons killed, the day before, near Colorado City. A large body of Indians also attacked the station at Hugo Springs, but were repulsed by the guards.

Above: *General George Crook learned his tactics from his Indian adversaries – who were often his friends. He was universally respected on the frontier in a career that spanned a quarter of a century, after his service in the Civil War.*

Against such threats hanging over settlers in the West, it was the cavalry above all who had to take action. But they operated in a maze of conflicting pressures: the demands of fearful settlers to wipe out the Indians once and for all; the demands of pro-Indian forces (of which there was a small but steady element) for justice and restraint; the political pressures to keep a good face on things, even when Indian land was blatantly being stolen. Surprisingly, it was sometimes the soldiers who were closest to the Indians and whose word was most trusted by their enemies – between soldier and Indian there was a certain bond of mutual respect and sometimes outright admiration. This peculiar situation is nowhere better seen than in the career of the greatest Indian fighter of all, General George Crook.

A West Point classmate and friend of Philip Sheridan's, Crook first went to Indian country in 1866 as an Indian commissioner in Oregon. In that booming territory, he developed the tactics that would lead him both to unprecedented victories over Indians and, paradoxically, to becoming one of their greatest friends and champions. To begin with, Crook had a genuine love for many of the Indian ways of life, which he studied tirelessly. He befriended the Indians, riding and eating with them. In contrast to most soldiers, he looked at his enemies as individuals, and quickly showed tribesmen that he was fair and honest; they knew George Crook would punish only the guilty and would always be willing to talk. He also studied everything about the countryside, making sure he knew the terrain, the biology, the botany. Thus on his campaigns Crook generally knew where to find game for his soldiers and grass for his horses.

But Crook's most original and controversial

MANULITO 1027

idea was his conviction that the best men to fight Indians were Indians. Whereas most cavalrymen used few Indian scouts in the West, Crook sometimes rode out with more Indian than white fighting men. He liked his Indian recruits wild, preferably right off the warpath, knowing that in most cases he could trust their word and their belief that fighting itself was an honorable occupation – for many, the most honorable. He offered the braves an alternative – to do what they liked best rather than to rot on the reservations or be hunted down by the army. Once on the trail of a hostile band, Crook and his companies of soldiers and Indians would dog the renegades relentlessly until they were worn down and caught. When hostiles knew Crook was on their trail, even the most belligerent would often turn themselves in, knowing that they could trust Crook for a fair deal.

Once Crook got renegades back on the reservation, he spared no effort to teach them to farm, and the results were sometimes spectacular. However, in so doing he frequently ran afoul of

Tonto Apaches. But soon the local tribes learned Crook's style; when some renegades attacked a stagecoach and murdered most of the passengers, Crook carefully determined who the perpetrators were and wiped out only their camp. By late 1872 he had pacified all the Indians in the area except for scattered bands of Apache holdouts. Against these he made another campaign into the mountains of Arizona.

His detachment of soldiers and Indians swept through the Tonto Basin in six columns. The men were ordered to flush any renegades, ride until their horses gave out, follow on foot until their feet gave out, then to crawl. Any word of surrender from the hostiles was to be honored. Just after Christmas, Apache scouts of Major Brown's column found the major group of hostiles holed up in a cliffside cave above the Salt River. Marching all night in the bitter cold, Brown's vanguard stumbled on the Indians dancing and opened fire, killing six; the rest of the hostiles bolted for their cave, which was protected by large boulders and well supplied with food and ammunition. Hungrier and colder than their opponents, the soldiers settled into a siege.

Unable to fire directly into the cave, the troopers began ricocheting shots off the roof; screams from inside told them that the bullets were finding marks. Concerned for the women and children in the cave, the troopers finally stopped firing and called for surrender. Their reply was an eerie wail from inside; the Apaches were singing their death chant. Directly after, 20 renegades charged the troopers. These were soon driven back with six killed; the troopers returned to ricocheting shots. The end came

Above: *One of General Crook's encampments during the wide-ranging Indian Wars.*

traders and the Indian Bureau, whose income from selling food to the Indians was reduced when their charges became farmers. As a result, civilian authorities had a depressing record of relocating successful farming tribes to areas that were impossible to farm – with the usual result that the starving victims went back on the warpath out of desperation, and more settlers and soldiers were butchered. All in all, it was to prove a dismal and disgraceful cycle of corruption and resulting violence.

Having made a good record in Oregon, Crook was sent to Arizona in 1871 as commander of the Department of Arizona. There the Apaches, perhaps the toughest and wildest tribe in the West, were on a major rampage. On arrival, Crook got together five companies of cavalry and some Apache scouts and headed out for the hostiles. (By no means all Apaches were renegades – a large group had been encamped at Fort Craig for two years waiting for an answer to their peace offer.) Crook moved his column east to Fort Apache, near the New Mexico border, learning about the countryside and Indian customs on the way, talking constantly with settlers and Indians. The campaign came to little this time – only a small skirmish with the

Right: *An Apache scout displays his Winchester '73 repeating rifle in this photograph by Timothy O'Sullivan, who also chronicled the Civil War.*

when another column of cavalry arrived and started shooting into the cave from above. Finally, there was silence from within. The troopers crept warily forward, finding, to their astonishment, 30 survivors; the women and children had hidden under stones and corpses. No braves were alive and unwounded. The Yellowlegs and their scouts headed back home, taking with them the captive women and children, leaving the dead where they lay.

By the end of a winter of hard campaigning, Crook had subdued all the Apaches except for a small band under Cochise. Then General Oliver O Howard arrived to become Crook's commanding officer. Howard made a deal with Cochise to stay on the reservation, and Crook got busy helping the Indians to dig an irrigation ditch and start farming. For all the braves' traditional belief that farming was effeminate, they proved to be superlative farmers indeed. Crook bought their considerable surplus for his troops. As usual, however, the Indian Bureau saw its prerogatives and profits threatened, and pressured President U S Grant to move the Apaches to a thoroughly arid reservation. Grant gave in, and the Apaches were forcibly relocated.

Crook, sure of what would happen, used his network of Indian friends and spies to keep up with developments. It was not long before the breakouts and depredations began. A band under Delt-chay murdered some ranchers, and Crook demanded the renegade's head from his Apache compatriots. They soon provided it – in

William S Soule's photograph of Little Big Mouth by his lodge'.

Right: *A Sioux reservation like the one that comprised 25 percent of Dakota Territory during Sheridan's 1876 campaign.*

Below: *Hunkpapa Sioux leader Sitting Bull, a medicine man who allied himself with Chiefs Crazy Horse, Gall, Rain in the Face and others to defeat the 7th Cavalry at Little Big Horn. Photograph by David Barry (1885).*

fact, two groups provided heads alleged to be Delt-chay's. Unsure which was the correct one, Crook duly paid for both. Confronting other hostiles, he made a typical offer: he couldn't kill them out of hand, he said, but he'd be delighted to give them a chance to run and then chase them down and kill them. Finally, the hostiles entreated him to allow surrender, to which Crook finally agreed. Given civilian policies, he knew the resulting peace was likely to be temporary. But for the moment peace there was, and Crook had brought it. By now the most successful Indian fighter in the country, known as 'the man who hires hostiles,' he was called on when the Sioux and Cheyenne rose up in the Dakotas in the spring of 1875. Philip Sheridan was about to start the greatest Indian campaign in history and he wanted George Crook to be part of it. In the end, though, Crook's contribution to the Sioux war was to be lost in the story of George Custer, who wanted the world to recognize him as the greatest of Indian fighters.

What lay behind the discontent of the Sioux and their Cheyenne allies was an all-too-common story. The Laramie Treaty of 1868 had given vast tracts of supposedly useless land in the Dakotas to these two tribes. But in 1874 Custer had pursued Indians into the Black Hills, the ancient sacred territory of the local tribes, and had come out crowing that the place was full of gold. Thus Custer drafted the death warrant for both Indian claims to the area and his own life. President Grant was persuaded to herd all the Indians in the area onto reservations and to declare any holdouts hostiles – all this in clear violation of the treaty. As usual, the human toll of such double-dealing was to be appalling.

Miners and fortune-hunters began moving into the Black Hills, crowding the Indians and shooting buffalo by the millions. At first, Sheridan's actions seemed to honor the treaty – Crook was ordered to get the miners and squatters out. Ominously, however, the miners were allowed to leave their claims staked. The significance of this was not lost on the Indians. A massive hostile alliance of Sioux and Cheyenne was already forming under two great leaders – Sitting Bull and Crazy Horse. Crook did the best he could; having turned the fierce Apaches into farmers, he was now asked to subdue Indians who only wanted to be left alone to farm.

Early in 1876 a Crook subordinate bungled an attack on Crazy Horse's village, letting the hostiles get away. Emboldened by this failure, more Sioux and Cheyenne took to the warpath. Finally Sheridan organized his big offensive. During April and May of 1876, three army columns were to converge into the territory of the Sioux and Cheyenne. The column leaders were Colonel John Gibbon, General Alfred H Terry and Crook. Terry's force consisted mainly of George Custer's 7th Cavalry, 600 strong. Custer himself had just returned from one of his periodic trips East to get himself into the papers.

Above: *Custer's discovery of the bodies of Lieutenant L S Kidder and his men at Beaver Creek, Kansas, in July 1867. Both Indians and cavalrymen stripped, scalped and otherwise mutilated their victims.*

Left: *Crazy Horse and his Sioux and Cheyenne warriors almost overwhelmed George Crook's cavalry at the Battle of the Rosebud River, 17 June 1876.*

In the process he had testified against some of Grant's relatives, accusing them of corruption, and had nearly found himself cashiered for insubordination.

On 9 June Crook's column – 15 companies of cavalry and 5 of infantry, plus a number of Indians – was attacked by Crazy Horse at the Tongue River. Crook had been expecting it: Crazy Horse had told him not to go there, and Crook knew this attack was mounted mainly to show that the Cheyenne chieftain kept his word. There were no US Army deaths in the attack. Crook continued, picking up a large party of Shoshone scouts (the Indian Bureau had forbidden him to use Sioux).

The next attack was not for show. On 17 June Crook's men were in camp at the Rosebud River, just north of the Wyoming-Montana border. Two Crow scouts rode into camp screaming 'Sioux! Sioux!' It was Crazy Horse, who had

Sargeant Carter Johnson's
F Troop, 3rd US Cavalry,
surveying the scene of
battle with a Cheyenne
force.

made a remarkable battle plan to annihilate Crook's force (he later told his adversary the details of the plan.) Crazy Horse first hit Crook with 1500 braves, only a fifth of his force. If the soldiers broke into detachments, as they usually did, the groups were to be crushed one at a time. However, if Crook stayed in one body, Crazy Horse planned to lure the soldiers into a box canyon and there fall upon them with his superior numbers. Knowing his opponent, Crook did neither. Instead, he put his horses in view of the Indians as bait; when the Indians headed for them, he picked them off with men stationed on the heights. The attack blunted, Crook advanced his line and drove the hostiles back.

Nonetheless, it had been a very close call, and Crook was shaken, his column badly hurt and out of supplies. There was no word from the forces of Terry and Custer, 50 miles away. Crook did not know it then, but he was essentially out of the war. Neither could he know that Crazy Horse and Sitting Bull had left him for a rendezvous with Custer and the 7th Cavalry.

For George Custer, it was a long road that had led him to the Little Big Horn. Despite graduating at the bottom of his West Point class, he was a general in the Union Army by the age of 23. Several things marked Custer from the beginning – his dandyish style (he had yards of braid on his uniform and long blond hair), his flair for publicity and his unquestioned bravery. Indeed, there were few braver men on earth than George Custer, though his was the type of impetuousness that often rushed in where angels feared. At the end of the war he married the beautiful Libby Sheridan; their wedding

present from Philip Sheridan was the table on which Lee had signed the surrender at Appomattox. In the victory parade after the Civil War, Custer had let his horse run away so he could get his cheers solo; it was an entirely characteristic stunt.

As a cavalry leader on the Plains, Custer quickly established a reputation of firmness bordering on cruelty – he had soldiers flogged, shot deserters, consigned miscreants to a hole in the ground. After serving in various commands with varied success (including a year's suspension, later revoked, for general mismanagement of his outfit), Custer was placed by his old mentor Sheridan at the head of the 7th Cavalry. Unlike Crook, Custer had little interest in understanding his enemies; thus he fit in well with Sheridan's all-but-genocidal policies. After the massacre of Black Kettle's tribe, Custer became (after Chivington) the white man most hated by the Cheyenne. One chief greeted Custer for a parley by smiling and handing him a pipe while denouncing him as a traitor and a murderer. Custer, who spoke no Cheyenne, thought he was being honored. Though Custer sometimes negotiated fairly with Indians – making sure the newpapers heard about it – he more often betrayed them.

At 30 Custer began a self-glorifying autobiography which he never finished, but his many articles were later collected into the popular book *My Life On The Plains*. He took frequent leaves to the East, where he was lionized as the great Indian fighter. Few of his superiors shared that enthusiasm. Though Sheridan remained warm, Crook detested Custer; another superior described him as 'cold-

blooded, untruthful, and unprincipled.' Despite Custer's harshness, however, his 7th Cavalry was a loyal and spirited outfit, ready to follow him anywhere. They knew he had a habit of riding in first and scouting things out later, but they relied on what they called 'Custer's Luck.'

As we saw, Custer's 600-man outfit was part of Terry's command in the offensive of spring 1876. At the beginning of June, Terry's men moved through the Dakotas toward a juncture with Gibbon's command; both were then to move out against Indian strongholds. After striking Crook's detachment in the middle of the month, Crazy Horse and Sitting Bull established a camp of 12,000 Indians from many tribes, but mostly Sioux and Cheyenne, in the river valley of the Little Big Horn.

Custer, who had almost been cashiered for insubordination and thereby missed his chance to command the entire column, was determined to operate independently of Terry and reclaim his reputation. Terry seemed to go along with that. He ordered Custer to command the main offensive force and, while advising Custer to advance to union with Gibbon, nonetheless added, 'unless you shall see sufficient reason for departing from [the orders].' With that provision Terry gave Custer free rein.

Custer and his men rode out into history. By 24 June he knew from his scouts about the Indian village on the Little Big Horn, but he still had no conception of how big it was. He decided to replay his attack on Black Kettle, charging into the village at dawn. On 25 June he took his troopers toward the village carefully, hoping for surprise. But soon he discovered Indian scouts on his trail and realized he had to attack immediately, in broad daylight, before the village pulled up and vanished. His experience said that the best way to destroy an encampment was to hit it from several sides at once. Accordingly, he detached Captain Frederick W Benteen with 115 men to mop up any villages to the south and then rejoin the main column in the valley of the Little Big Horn.

Custer and the remainder rode on for a couple of hours; the 135 men of Company B lagged behind inexcusably – providentially for their own lives. Then a scout reported to Custer that the village seemed to be pulling up stakes (which was incorrect). Based on this information, Custer hurried to deploy the attack, ordering a detachment of 140 men and 35 Indian scouts under Major Marcus A Reno to assault the lower end of the village. Now he had stripped away the bulk of his column. Custer and his two remaining battalions headed north to close in on the village's upper end. With him was his younger brother, Captain Tom Custer.

In the middle of the afternoon, Major Reno caught sight of the village and was astonished at its extent – a procession of teepees stretching three miles down the river. Therefore, rather than riding in shooting, Reno ordered his men to dismount and form a skirmish line. Before long they were surrounded by a swarm of warriors: the situation quickly proved hopeless. Across the way Reno could see Custer's companies riding on the bluffs, too far away to come to their aid. Reno's men pulled back into some woods as the attack grew fiercer. Finally, one of Reno's scouts was shot as he stood beside the Major; rattled, with the scout's brains splattered over him, Reno shouted contradictory orders to his men. Soon they were fleeing for their lives toward the river. Indian warriors rode beside them and shot into the troopers at will. Reno's command reached the heights above the river with 90 casualties out of 175 troopers and scouts.

There what was left of the command was joined by Benteen and his three companies. Hearing the news, Benteen decided to stay put and let Custer fend for himself. Apparently it occurred to no one that Custer might not be able to fend for himself. Custer's luck remained unquestioned.

But by then that luck was already running out fast. An hour before, Custer's adjutant, W W Cooke, had scribbled a note: 'Benteen – Come on. Big village. Be quick. Bring packs. P.S. Bring pacs.' (sic) It was the last word anyone would hear from the doomed column. Carrying it to Benteen, the courier – whose luck had not run out – passed Boston Custer, who was riding toward the column. Boston made it in time to join his two brothers in death. By the time Custer's command was descending into the valley toward the village, the Indians were galloping over to meet it after their rout of Reno. Assuming that Reno was engaged at the bottom of the village and Benteen approaching, Custer rode in confidently.

No white man would live to tell the tale of what ensued that 25th of July. But Indian accounts and careful archaeology have revealed some of the story of Custer's last stand. The Indians struck Custer's left and rear, driving him up onto a low ridge where there was no shelter at all. There, in five clumps, the 210 troopers made their stand. The Indians closed in, their war cries filling the air. A chief named Low Dog called to his men, 'This is a good day to die: Follow me!' Another named Wooden Leg remembered the advance: 'The shooting at first was at a distance, but we kept creeping in closer all around the ridge. A warrior would jump up, shoot, jerk himself down quickly, then crawl forward a little farther.' Contrary to later depictions of the fight, few of the Indians were mounted. Before long they had stampeded or killed all the troopers' horses, stranding the men on the ridge.

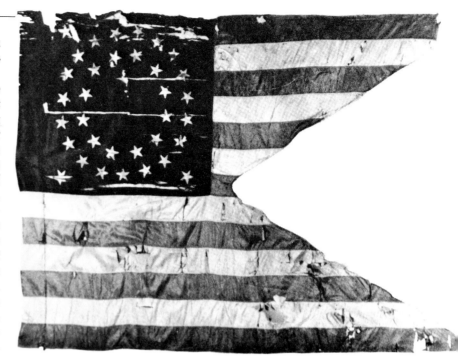

Opposite, top: *Guidon of the 7th Cavalry, used to indicate the position of a troop in battle, retrieved from the field at Little Big Horn.*

Right: *Cavalrymen rest and recover from a skirmish in defense of a wagon train in this scene by Remington.*

Below: *An imaginative recreation of Custer's last stand: no white man returned to describe the Battle of the Little Big Horn. On the right is Chief Low Dog, who survived the battle with most of his warriors.*

The end came very fast. As the men were picked off one by one, Custer's north flank began to crumple. Chief Lame White Man led his men to the charge, shouting, 'Come! We can kill all of them!' Crazy Horse himself led an attack on the clump of men around George Custer, who, already mortally wounded, had barricaded himself behind dead horses under his regimental pennant. An Indian described the last few moments of resistance: 'Horses were running over the soldiers and over each other. The fighting was really close, and they were shooting almost without taking aim.' A few soldiers made a desperate run for the river; they were quickly cut down. Then, as Wooden Leg remembered, 'The shots quit coming from the soldiers.' As the Indians crept forward through the bodies of horses and men, a dying trooper suddenly rose on one arm, holding the Indians at bay with his revolver. A Sioux tore the gun away and shot the trooper in the head. Then the only sound was the victory cries of the Indians. It had taken less than an hour for George Custer to preside over one of the worst defeats in American history. The gods' great joke on him was that in so doing he finally achieved the immortal fame he had craved so long.

Crazy Horse was not finished with the 7th Cavalry – in fact, he had no idea that he had killed its commander. The Indians rode back and besieged Benteen and Reno for the rest of 25 June and into the evening of the next day. The terrified and exhausted troopers held out, in growing alarm at Custer's failure to appear. By dawn of the 27th, the Indians were gone and the men saw the approach of Terry's and Gibbon's column. Together they rode to find out what had become of Custer. At the Little Big Horn they found something from their worst nightmares. It was more than death, it was a scene of horror that would haunt them the rest of their lives. Most of the bodies had been mutilated, many beyond recognition. George Custer himself was stripped of his buckskins but otherwise untouched except for the two bullet wounds that had killed him. That he was not mutilated like the others was probably an accident; none of these Indians knew Custer by sight, and his famous long yellow hair had been cut short just before the campaign. Most of the dead were buried on the spot in shallow graves. As always, the Indians had carried off their own dead, who have been estimated at fewer than 50. One survivor was found: a wounded cavalry horse named 'Comanche,' who lived on until 1891 as the pampered mascot of the 7th Cavalry.

At a Court of Inquiry that was convened to examine the disaster, Captain Benteen provided a remarkably frank post-mortem: 'There were a great deal too many Indians who were powerful good shots on the other side. We were at their hearths and homes – and they were fighting for all the good God gives anyone to fight for.'

The Indians did not keep fighting for long. Sheridan began assembling every soldier he could get his hands on to crush the Sioux and Cheyenne revolt. Before another year had passed, the hostiles were driven back onto reservations.

Elsewhere, the cavalry continued their operations. One of the saddest episodes of the Indian wars came in 1877, with the Nez Percé rebellion

Below, right: Chief Spotted Tail, a friend of General George Crook's, conferring with Sheridan and his subordinates.

Below: Chief Joseph of the Nez Percés, who led a doomed uprising against Indian Bureau expulsion of his people from their Oregon homeland.

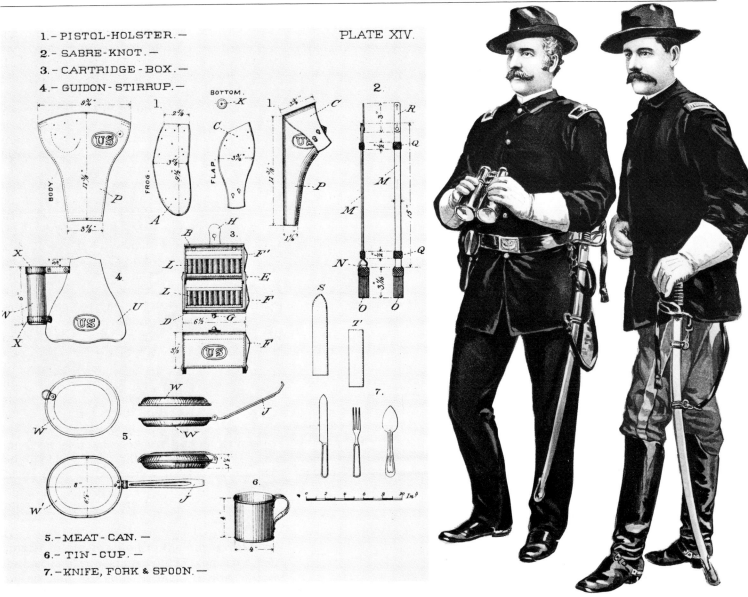

1.- PISTOL-HOLSTER.-
2.- SABRE-KNOT.-
3.- CARTRIDGE-BOX.-
4.- GUIDON-STIRRUP.-

PLATE XIV.

5.- MEAT-CAN.-
6.- TIN-CUP.-
7.- KNIFE, FORK & SPOON.-

Above: Cavalry accoutrements and campaign dress of the early 1890s: Brigadier General and Line Officer.

in Oregon. The tribe had always been peaceful, was among the first to be Christianized, and boasted that its members had never killed a white man. All this did not save the Nez Percé from white depredations: settlers had begun crowding onto their Wallowa Valley territory. Finally, corrupt Indian agents tried to remove the Nez Percé, and 450 braves under the extraordinary Chief Joseph went on the warpath. As always, the Army was called in to finish dirty work begun by the Indian Bureau. General O O Howard struck the Nez Percé in July; they melted into the hills, reappearing at Big Hole Basin. There John Gibbon attacked them with 200 men, who made little headway before the Indians melted away again, racing for the Canadian border. In the Bear Paw Mountains, only 40 miles from the border, General Nelson A Miles caught up with them and attacked with six companies of troopers and five of infantry. Chief Joseph, commanding only about a hundred warriors by then, fought for four days before surrendering. In 11 weeks the Nez Percé had fought 13 engagements with 10 Army outfits and had traveled 1600 miles. In his unforgettable words of surrender, Chief Joseph epitomized the whole tragedy of the American Indian:

Tell General Howard that I know his heart. . . . I am tired of fighting. Our chiefs are killed. It is cold and we have no blankets. The little children are freezing to death. My people – some of them – have run away to the hills, and we have no blankets, no food. . . . I want to have time to look for my children and to see how many of them I can find; maybe I shall find them among the dead. Hear me, my chiefs: my heart is sick and sad. From where the sun now stands, I will fight no more forever.

Despite years of joint effort by Chief Joseph and General Howard, the Nez Percé were never allowed to return to their homeland.

In the West, after the Little Big Horn disaster, the fighting continued. Crazy Horse's alliance evaporated, some going to Canada with Sitting Bull, others to the Black Hills with Crazy Horse. Spurned by their former allies the Sioux, the Cheyenne made peace with Crook, by then in charge of the Indian agencies in the Black Hills. Crook sent his Indian friend Chief Spotted Tail to reason with Crazy Horse, who finally gave up in May of 1877. Then the government broke the promises Crook had made; despite Crook's

vehement objections, the Sioux were ordered to be relocated. Crazy Horse broke out with a few braves, but was soon rounded up by cavalry. The great Sioux chief was killed while under arrest, in the usual mysterious circumstances attending the deaths of captured chiefs. For several years there was a period of relative calm on the Plains. Then, in 1882, the Apaches went back on the warpath in Arizona and New Mexico.

Clearly it was a job for George Cook, and he was called back to Arizona. He had seen it all before – the massacres, the rapes, the hideous tortures inflicted on captives. Crook had written, 'The Apache is the tiger of the human species.' It was an apt description: lean, sinewy and tireless, Apache warriors had preyed on neighboring tribes for centuries. On his faithful mule 'Apache', Crook rode into the Arizona mountains, questioning Indian friends and hearing their complaints. He heard the familiar stories of white encroachment and Indian Bureau corruption. After chasing away the whites from Indian land, Crook persuaded most of the Apaches to return to the reservation. But a group including Chief Geronimo remained at large, leading a band that raided out of Mexico. Geronimo had hated whites since Mexicans killed his mother, wife and three children.

Under a new treaty that allowed Americans to pursue a hot Indian trail into Mexico, Crook took out after the 200 renegades in May 1883. To everyone's surprise, the hostiles gave up without a fight in the Sierra Madre Mountains. Perhaps they were discouraged by the fact that

Below: *Kiowa Chief White Bear (called Satanta) died by his own hand in 1878, several years after this photograph was taken by William S Soule.*

200 of Crook's 250 men were Apaches. All the hostiles settled down to the reservation and Geronimo proved an enthusiastic farmer. There was peace for two years. But then an old pattern was repeated when Indian agents bridled at Crook's buying the surplus food raised by the Indians. Amid rising tensions, Geronimo went on a drinking binge in May 1885 and then bolted with a few braves, heading for Mexico. Before reaching the border they killed 73 civilians and soldiers.

One of Crook's officers summed up the cavalry's problem from his own first-hand experience on the frontier.

Here is an enemy with a thousand miles of hilly and sandy country to run over, and each brave provided with from three to five ponies trained like dogs. They carry almost nothing but arms and ammunition; they can live on cactus; they can go more than forty-eight hours without water; they know every water-hole and every foot of ground in this vast extent of country; they have incredible powers of endurance; they run in small bands, scattering at the first indications of pursuit. . . . One week of such work will kill the average soldier and his horse; the Apache thrives on it.

But Crook found Geronimo's trail and latched onto it with his usual tenacity. Leaving Fort Bowie in December of 1885, he marched with two detachments comprised mainly of Indians, many of them Apaches. By 9 January an Indian scout of Captain Emmett Crawford's, commanding Crook's main column, had located Geronimo's hideout deep in the Mexican mountains. By marching all night, the cavalrymen and scouts made it to the hideout next day. There they confronted not only Geronimo, who immediately made peace overtures, but also a detachment of Mexican soldiers. The latter happened to be Tarahumari Indians and old foes of the Apaches. In a confused encounter the Mexicans fired on Crawford's scouts; instead of Apaches, they hit and killed Crawford. A shoot-out followed between American and Mexican forces, while Geronimo and his men watched with interest. Soon the situation calmed down, though not without deaths on both sides, and Geronimo agreed to return to the reservation. But the unpredictable old chief dallied in returning and public censure of Crook mounted; he was excoriated for taking an Indian's word. Finally, Crook and Geronimo sat down for a tense face-to-face session and the chief agreed again to surrender. But the old Indian could not sit still: soon he was drunk again and riding the range. To Sheridan's angry protest, Crook said he was convinced the chief would return when he sobered up; in any event, Crook would do things his own way or be relieved. Sheridan thereupon relieved him, replacing him with General Nelson A Miles.

It was the end of Crook's Indian fighting career; he had been sunk by his trust of his enemies. Now less sympathetic soldiers would take over the business. Miles chased Geronimo ineffectually for a while with 5000 troopers – the renegades numbered about 80. Finally, an ex-subordinate of Crook's talked the Indians into surrendering. The wily and hard-drinking old Geronimo survived to ride in a state coach in Theodore Roosevelt's inaugural parade; his name survived still longer as a jumping call of US paratroopers. Crook retired East, only to return as head of the Missouri Division, a desk job he filled honorably until 1890.

Crook's death is one reason the year 1890 is considered the point at which the Indian wars came to a close, and with them the American frontier era. Another reason is that December of that year saw the last and one of the most devastating major encounters between Indians and horse soldiers – at Wounded Knee, South Dakota. Among Plains Indians there had grown up a mystical movement called the Ghost Shirt Dance: its adherents believed that by dancing in magical shirts, they could become invulnerable to bullets, make the whites go away and re-surrect the buffalo. Clearly, it was a sect born of desperation and despair. By 1890 the movement was widespread, and the Oglala Sioux and other tribes, all of them near starvation on the

Top: *Geronimo and his Chiracahua Apaches confront their pursuers on an Arizona ridge studded with spiky yucca.*

Above: *Troop A of the 6th US Cavalry on the Mexican border during the Geronimo campaign (1885).*

Above: *Arapaho women performing the Ghost Shirt Dance, a cult ritual that sought to allay Indian despair by an appeal to the powers of magic.*

Main picture: *Frozen bodies strewn over the battlefield at Wounded Knee, South Dakota, 29 December 1890.*

Inset: *The 7th Cavalry officers who sought to revenge Custer at Wounded Knee – and added a sorry chapter to American history.*

government dole, were becoming belligerent. In December General Miles began accumulating troops in the area of Wounded Knee and ordered the arrest of Sitting Bull, who was then camped nearby (and who had nothing to do with the agitation). Like his great partner Crazy Horse, Sitting Bull was killed during arrest under 'mysterious circumstances.'

This triggered a rampage among Big Foot's Oglalas and other Ghost Dancers in the area, during which Big Foot tried to flee with his starving village. The 7th Cavalry was detailed to round them up, take them back to Wounded Knee and there disarm them. As that was being done, a shot was fired – by nobody knows whom. It was all the excuse the 7th needed; they emptied their rifles and four machine guns into the largely unarmed Indians. Within a few moments Big Foot and over 200 others were mowed down. The 7th Cavalry had gotten its revenge for George Custer – and added a disgrace to its history. In the ensuing outbreak of Indian rage, the 7th had to be rescued by the Buffalo Troopers. The outbreak was soon squelched: the Indians were too hungry and weak to fight for long.

There were to be further actions against small groups of hostiles here and there, but Wounded Knee was the bitter end of a bitter struggle. Now America was settled from coast to coast and 'safe' from Indians. It seemed the result of an irresistible destiny. For 25 years the Yellowlegs had done their last big job bravely, for well and for ill. At times, paradoxically, they had been the best friends the Indians had. In any case, the recriminations remained for history to decide, and the horse cavalry moved on to its last exploits, which would be mainly footnotes to history. But Wounded Knee opened one new chapter in the American drama – a national Indian political movement.

The Cavalry Moves into the Twentieth Century

Previous pages:
American forces (Rough Riders in foreground) hoist their flag after the surrender of Santiago, Cuba, in the Spanish–American War.

Below: *Cavalry officer and enlisted men in turn-of-the-century full-dress uniforms.*

Bottom: *This 2nd-Cavalry mount was a 23-year veteran when he was retired in 1897.*

With the final defeat of the Sioux at Wounded Knee and the disappearance of the American frontier, America began directing some of its energies beyond its borders in a movement destined to see the United States emerge as a world power. Few periods in American history have witnessed such rapid technological growth and such fundamental change in national policy.

For the US Cavalry, the years following the Indian Wars saw some basic improvements. In addition to new drill regulations, already underway, the Regular Cavalry and one regiment of Volunteers were equipped with the .30-caliber Krag-Jörgensen magazine carbine, sporting a cartridge containing smokeless powder and a muzzle velocity of about 2000 feet per second. And for the first time in nearly 50 years, peace reigned in the American West. After Wounded Knee troopers continued to patrol the plains and mountains and track down renegades, but only two minor Indian rebellions required more serious cavalry attention, and neither approached a major encounter. In 1898 the Chippewas of Minnesota had a small skirmish with troopers, and in 1907, when the Utes in Colorado and Utah refused to send their children to school, the entire 6th Cavalry regiment was sent to play truant officer and enforce the law. Veterans remarked that the sympathies of the troopers appeared to be with the children whom they dragged in kicking and screaming to education and civilization. But before the mounted service settled too comfortably into the routine of garrison life, civil troubles erupted in the cities and industrial centers of the rapidly expanding nation. Between 1886 and 1895, the US Army intervened in 328 labor disputes and related disturbances in 49 states and territories, and the horse soldier was often called upon to preserve order. But the next real fighting the cavalry saw came with the Spanish-American War in 1898.

By then the cavalry, with its unequaled tradition and proud officers and men, had become the top choice of many high-ranking cadets at West Point, and was clearly the glamor organization of the US Army. Even so, technological progress was making the horse obsolete. While the internal-combustion engine was preparing to burst upon the scene to alter the face – and the course – of civilization, the range, accuracy and rapidity of modern arms placed cavalry in a position inferior to that of artillery and infantry. With machine guns able to stop a cavalry charge at 2000 yards and artillery at 3500, frontal assault by horse troops was a thing of the past; indeed, the Napoleonic Wars were the last in which horsed cavalry were used as the principal assault troops on a battlefield. In Europe, the use of heavy or assault cavalry, a product of feudalism and chivalry, died hard in Europe in the face of rifles and machine guns. American cavalrymen, however, acknowledging the effects of modern weapons, asserted that

Below: *First Cavalrymen at Fort Grant, Arizona, pass their off-duty hours playing draw poker.*

the mounted arm was still essential, and proved it by employing cavalry in flanking, screening and reconnaissance, and in the guerrilla-style tactics used against the Indians of the West. With artillery taking over the function of heavy cavalry in attack, and modern armored mechanized mounts – that is, tanks – still decades away, infantry might be the most important arm on the field of battle. But it was cavalry that guarded the ammunition, screened, foraged and provided the information necessary to conduct battles. Especially in the 1890s, reconnaissance gained importance. American cavalry, trained to fight mounted and dismounted – combining dismounted fire with the mounted charge – preserved its mobility while adding the firepower of modern infantry.

When insurrection broke out on the island of Cuba in 1895, the American people, who could be expected to favor the aspirations of colonials for independence, sympathized with the insurgents. Their support grew the following year, when newly appointed Spanish governor General Valeriano Weyler attempted to stifle the rebellion by herding noncombatant men, women and children into concentration camps and garrisoned towns where they died by thousands for lack of proper provisioning. Despite rising American public opinion, neither President Grover Cleveland nor his successor William McKinley favored intervention.

151

America really had no foreign policy, but publication of a letter written by the Spanish minister to the United States, which characterized President McKinley as 'a weakling,' and the 1898 sinking of the US battleship *Maine*, in which 260 Americans lost their lives, gave interventionists the upper hand. Newspapers cried 'Remember the *Maine*!' and the nation sang 'There'll Be a Hot Time in the Old Town Tonight.' An ultimatum was sent to Spain on 27 March 1898; the Spanish Government appeared willing to honor it, but the American people could not wait. Congress passed a joint resolution on 19 April 1898 proclaiming Cuba free and authorizing the president to use force to expel the Spaniards.

The US Cavalry of 1898 was not prepared for war. There were 27,000 enlisted men in the whole US Army, of whom something less than 6000 were cavalrymen. Part of the 3rd Cavalry was at Fort Ethan Allen, Vermont, and part of the 6th at Fort Meyer, Virginia, but most troopers were thinly spread across garrisons in Montana,

Above: *Theodore Roosevelt and his Rough Riders on San Juan Hill, Cuba: Colonel Roosevelt was, in fact, the only man mounted for the famous charge against this objective.*

Opposite: *The inflammatory journalism of William Randolph Hearst and Joseph Pulitzer was a causative factor in the Spanish–American War.*

Below: *The true cause of the explosion that destroyed the battleship* Maine *in Havana Harbor was never determined. Some experts held that the explosion was internal and not attributable to a Spanish mine, as the Americans had charged.*

The World.

WORLDS CIRCULATED YESTERDAY   "Circulation Books Open to All."   "Circulation Books Open to All."   WORLDS CIRCULATED YEERDAY

VOL. XXXVIII. NO. 13,430.   NEW YORK, THURSDAY, FEBRUARY 17, 1898.   PRICE

MAINE EXPLOSION CAUSED BY BOMB OR TORPEDO?

.apt. Sigsbee and Consul-General Lee Are in Doubt---The World Has Sent a
Special Tug, With Submarine Divers, to Havana to Find Out---Lee Asks
for an Immediate Court of Inquiry---260 Men Dead.

IN A SUPPRESSED DESPATCH TO THE STATE DEPARTMENT, THE CAPTAIN SAYS THE ACCIDENT WAS MADE POSSIBLE BY AN ENEMY.

Dr. E. C. Pendleton, Just Arrived from Havana, Says He Overheard Talk There of a Plot to Blow Up the Ship---
Zalinski, the Dynamite Expert, and Other Experts Report to The World that the Wreck Was Not
Accidental---Washington Officials Ready for Vigorous Action if Spanish Responsibility
Can Be Shown---Divers to Be Sent Down to Make Careful Examinations.

Wyoming, Colorado, Kansas and other points widely scattered throughout the West. To add to their numbers, a Congressional Act of 26 April 1898 authorized the Regular Cavalry to reactivate two troops in each regiment (from troops deactivated in 1890 or last filled with Indians), and to add a lieutenant, a sergeant, four corporals and 34 privates to each troop. This brought troop strength to 104 and regiment strength to 1262 officers and men. To further increase cavalry power, State Organized Militia units and special Volunteer units were also authorized to muster. This resulted in the formation of three volunteer regiments, only one of which, the 1st United States Volunteer Cavalry, saw action in the war with Spain.

The 1st United States Volunteer Cavalry, also known as the Rough Riders or 'Teddy's Terrors' was created by then Assistant Secretary of the Navy Theodore Roosevelt. It was the last of the 'personal regiments' – elite units raised and officered by a prominent civilian for a particular war, and one of six cavalry regiments active in the West Indies. All cavalry in Cuba fought dismounted: the only man mounted in the historic charge of San Juan Hill was Colonel Roosevelt, and he had to dismount at a wire fence and lead his men to the summit on foot. The charismatic Roosevelt and his colorful troopers captured the imagination of a nation (as well as the interest and attention of the leading war correspondents) that looked upon this war as a glorious national picnic that nearly everyone wanted to attend. Almost forgotten is the role played by then Captain John Joseph Pershing, who guided the 2nd Squadron of the 10th Cavalry up San Juan Hill and earned a Silver Star and a brevet as Major of Volunteers on his way to one of the most distinguished military careers in American history.

So popular was Roosevelt that when news went out that he was forming a regiment, the ranks were filled in less than three weeks (994 enlisted men and 47 officers). Roosevelt chose to serve as lieutenant colonel, second-in-command to his friend Colonel Leonard Wood, Apache fighter and competent Regular medical officer. Principally composed of cowboys and polo players, the Rough Riders also included actors, New York policemen, doctors, frontier sheriffs, prospectors, society leaders, professional gamblers and college athletes. All could ride and shoot. They assembled at a training camp at San Antonio, Texas, in May 1898, and within 13 days the officers organized, equipped and trained a full regiment of horse soldiers – an operation Regular Cavalry outfits were expected to perform in 13 weeks. The Rough Riders shot out lights in local saloons, and at the end of May a high-ranking Regular officer, in whose honor a dress review had been scrupulously prepared, remarked that he had never seen anything worse in his life. In the rush to get to the scene of action, there was no time to procure uniforms, and the regiment at first wore the canvas stable dress of the Regular Cavalry. By the time they reached Cuba, most dressed in the new regulation uniform, which at the time consisted of khaki breeches and blouses with blue flannel shirts (the only remnant of the old all-blue outfit). The Rough Riders wore red bandanas around their necks. Each trooper was armed with a magazine carbine and a six-shooter revolver. On 29 May the Rough Riders and 1100 horses and mules boarded trains for Tampa, Florida.

The confusion and mismanagement at Tampa was unbelievable. Legend says the regiment had to hold up trains at pistol point to obtain transportation to the docks; history records that they embarked for Cuba by seizing, boarding and holding an unguarded transport which had been assigned to two other regiments. Only eight troops of the Rough Riders ever got on board, and all the horses except those of the high-ranking officers were left behind.

The confusion at Tampa mirrored the confusion at higher levels. The Army had no true general staff, and the United States was preparing to go to war without any co-ordinated plan, without any knowledge of the strength and disposition of either the Spaniards or the Cuban insurgents, without joint Army-Navy planning for an attack on a hostile shore and without any accurate maps of Cuba. If the Spaniards had not been even more inept, the consequences for the United States would have been disastrous beyond imagination.

After sitting for several days in the stifling heat of Tampa Harbor, the American convoy got underway, landing on 22 June at Daiquiri, 18 miles east of Santiago Bay. The plan was to drive into the interior to take Santiago from the rear. The landing, which should have taken hours, took days, and would have been a catastrophe if the Spaniards had organized a determined resistance. Horses were transported ashore by throwing them overboard and letting them swim; several, including one of Colonel Roosevelt's, headed out to sea and drowned. Units got ashore as best they could; at least two men drowned.

After landing safely, the Rough Riders became part of the dismounted cavalry division under former Confederate cavalryman Major General Joseph Wheeler, who had for many years been forbidden to serve in the US Army (in the heat of battle he was heard to refer to the Spaniards as 'damn Yankees'). Wheeler's division consisted of about 3000 troopers composed from the Regular 1st, 3rd, 6th, 9th and 10th Cavalry and the Rough Riders. The 9th and 10th Cavalry were black regiments. Sabers were left behind with the horses, and all fought as infantry, with carbine and revolver. After regrouping, the division pushed ahead on foot into the dense jungle, running into the rear guard of a retiring Spanish force at Las Guasimas on 24 June. There 964 Americans engaged the enemy, winning a victory, with 16 troopers killed and 52 wounded, 8 of the dead and 34 of the wounded being Rough Riders. But the Spaniards had no intention of making a serious stand beyond the outer defenses of Santiago, the most important of which were a long series of ridges known collectively as San Juan. One week later, on 1 July

A troop transport ship loading troops for the war zone in Cuba, 1898.

Top left: *The capture of El Caney, El Paso and the fortifications at Santiago.*

Top right: *Assistant Secretary of the Navy, later President, Theodore Roosevelt was an avid outdoorsman despite asthmatic attacks so severe that he almost died in early childhood.*

Above; *Over half the 35,000 American troops who returned from Cuba had to be treated for malaria, typhoid fever and other tropical diseases at this quarantine camp at Montauk Point, Long Island.*

1898, while the American infantry concentrated on taking the village of El Caney and San Juan Heights, the dismounted cavalry, by way of diversion, stormed the strongly fortified Kettle Hill – the famous San Juan Hill. The Rough Riders dashed ahead of the Regulars of the 1st and 9th Cavalry and caught the first fire from the veteran Spanish infantry's modern Mauser rifles. The Regulars joined the Rough Riders for the final spurt, and the hill was taken. Despite comic-opera overtones, it was a tough fight with heavy losses. Eighty-nine of 490 Rough Riders were killed or wounded, and 375 troopers of 2300 cavalrymen engaged were killed or wounded. Santiago soon surrendered, and all fighting ended in September.

One squadron composed of troops from the 2nd Cavalry mounted on local horses escorted batteries and trains to the front lines at El Caney, and some troopers acted as couriers and litter bearers. In Puerto Rico, Troops A and C of the New York Volunteer Cavalry, also mounted, assisted in a conquest in which there was little bloodshed, no serious hardship and much fun. The Puerto Rican population as a whole received the American troops with enthusiasm.

The Army in Cuba met its worst problems after Santiago surrendered. Malaria, typhoid, yellow fever and unwholesome rations combined to cause such a problem that all American troops, including the Rough Riders, were brought back to an isolated camp on Montauk Point, Long Island, to recuperate. Of the 35,000 who passed through the camp, 20,000 were sick, but most recovered. The Rough Riders were lionized in New York City before being mustered out on 15 September 1898. They presented Roosevelt, who had been promoted to a full colonel shortly before the battle of San Juan Hill, with 'the Bronco Buster,' a statuette specially commissioned from Frederic Remington. So ended the last US Cavalry action of the 19th century.

While the fighting was going on in Cuba, America landed an expeditionary force of about 10,000 men in the Philippines, where native insurgents under their leader Emilio Aguinaldo were attempting to throw off the yoke of Spanish rule. Most Americans had no idea where the Philippines were, and were equally unprepared for the idea of a 6000-mile expedition into the Orient and the establishment of a colonial possession there. Commanded by Major General Wesley Merritt, a cavalryman who had served with distinction under Sheridan during the Civil War, the last military action of the war with Spain was undertaken by infantry who captured the city of Manila in mid-August. Merritt became the first American military governor of the Philippines.

Above: *The burning of Manila culminated America's first foray into the Philippines, where cavalryman Major General Wesley Merritt, a Civil War veteran, became the American military governor.*

No cavalry units went to the Philippines in 1898, but, largely at the urging of Major General Wheeler, who went to the Philippines after Cuba, cavalry began to arrive in 1899. By that fall most of the 4th Cavalry had reached the Philippines, and by June 1901, eight Regular cavalry regiments were employed there. After Manila, it had become apparent to the Filipino insurgents that the Americans were there to stay, and early in 1899 they turned against their former allies as they had against Spain. General Wheeler felt cavalry would be more useful in the guerrilla warfare which broke out throughout the islands. In addition to the Regulars, the 11th US Volunteer Cavalry, composed mostly of Americans already in the Philippines, was organized in Manila in the late summer of 1899, and a squadron of volunteer cavalry (eventually known as the Philippine Scouts) was raised among the Filipinos. Aguinaldo's insurrection was primarily a second lieutenant's war, characterized by constant fighting among small units in the jungle and back country. The fighting was bitter and brutal. Between May 1900 and June 1901, the Army fought over 1000 separate engagements in which little quarter was given or asked; casualties were high. Aguinaldo was captured in March 1901.

Aguinaldo's movement had occurred among the Christian Filipinos of the northern islands, led by the Christian tribe called the Tagalogs. No sooner had the Christian insurgents been subdued than the Muslim Moros of the southern islands rebelled. The Moros were fanatic warriors, hostile to all Christians and heirs of the belief that death in battle against the unbelievers ensured entry into paradise. They were veteran campaigners who had never surrendered some parts of the islands to Spain, and had fought for years against both the Spaniards and the Filipinos. They delayed attacking the Americans because they did not recognize them as Christians.

Under his various titles of Adjutant General, Chief Engineer, Chief Ordnance Officer, Chief Signalman, Captain and Brevet Major, John J Pershing led one of two successful cavalry expeditions into the heart of Moro land. Pershing had learned from fighting Apaches and leading Sioux scouts how important it was to understand the enemy. His knowledge of the Moros – he had taken the time to learn Moro – landed him an important command, and he employed mounted and dismounted cavalry supported by field artillery – howitzers or 'jackass artillery' carried on muleback – to subdue sultanate after sultanate, even in regions that had never heard of Americans or Spaniards. On one occasion he coerced the sultans into signing a peace treaty by threatening to spatter them with pig blood – a defilement that would prevent their entry into paradise. His command of the cavalry gained him the respect of his enemies, who appointed him honorary father of Moro aristocracy and *datu*, or prince, of the Muslim faith. Thirsty for news because the Army was doing its best to censor the American betrayal of Aguinaldo and his government, the media of the day built Pershing into an international hero. President Teddy Roosevelt, who

Opposite top: *General John J Pershing (1860–1948), as painted by Sir William Orpen.*

Above: *The cavalry's second excursion into the Orient came in 1901, when the 6th was dispatched to China as part of an international force to subdue the Boxer Rebellion. These prisoners near Tientsin were brought in by 6th Cavalry troopers.*

could appreciate a competent cavalryman, promoted him to brigadier general over the heads of 862 superior officers. In 1906 he was given command of Fort McKinley, becoming military governor of Mindanao in 1910, from which post he successfully controlled the restless Moros with cavalry, dismounted cavalry and infantry until a permanent peace was achieved in 1913. The Moros, awed by his merciless slaughter of their warriors at Mount Bagsak, where he had used mounted Philippine Scouts to screen combatants from the women and children so that his men could attack without quarter, had by then promoted him from Datu to Sultan Pershing.

Meanwhile, the US Cavalry was instrumental in putting down the Boxer Rebellion in China. At the turn of the century, many Chinese had accepted the teachings of the 'Boxers' (literally, 'the Righteous and Harmonious Fists'), fanatical members of a secret society dedicated to the extermination of 'foreign devils' and the eradication of their influence. The Boxers and their supporters killed hundreds of Westerners and Christian Chinese. After the German minister was murdered on 20 June 1900, and most foreigners took refuge in the British legation compound in Peking, they were besieged by a force that included some Chinese regular troops. A relief expedition was formed, with American, British, French, Japanese and Russian troops. Major General Adna Ramanza Chaffee, Indian fighter and Civil War cavalryman, commanded the American contingent, which included two squadrons of the 6th Cavalry (most of a regiment) – the same regiment in which he had enlisted as a private in 1861. The 3rd Squadron formed part of the force that stormed the walls of 'the Forbidden City' at Peking, becoming the first white troops to enter the city. This was the first war since the American Revolution in which the Army had co-operated with allies. The Spanish–American War painfully revealed US military inadequacies, but the American role in quelling the trouble in China – made possible by American proximity in the Philippines and involving relatively few troops – was great enough to establish the United States as a strong voice in future Far Eastern problems.

With the end of occupation duties in the Philippines nowhere in sight, Congress authorized an increase in the Regular Army in February 1901. Five new regiments were added to the cavalry, the 11th through the 15th, and enlisted troop strength was authorized to vary from 100 to 164, as directed by the President, the commander-in-chief. Units within the United States were kept to the minimum, while those in the islands were increased as necessary. The cavalry again enjoyed almost a decade of peaceful garrison routine, while regiments took turns serving in the Philippines, Hawaii, Panama and at various stations within the United States, primarily in the West. In between various experiments in cavalry reorganization and employment, a great deal of polo was played, improving horsemanship and the breeding of mounts. In 1904 the Krag-Jörgensen rifle of the Spanish-American War was replaced by the improved bolt-action, magazine-type Springfield 1903, which remained the infantry standard until the beginning of World War II. The Colt automatic .45-caliber pistol was approved in 1911. By the time of the Punitive Expedition into Mexico, all troopers in the United States were armed with it. In 1906 a machine-gun platoon commanded by a commissioned officer was added to each regiment, and during this period the all-khaki or olive-drab uniform became regulation and the blue

shirt of the Spanish-American War, the last remnant of the all-blue uniform, finally disappeared.

As of 30 June 1915, more than seven full regiments, about one-half of the cavalry, were serving on the Mexican border, as they had been since shortly after the 1910 abdication of Mexican President Porfirio Díaz. Unsettled conditions in Mexico caused by factions vying for power threatened to flow across the border. Two regiments were serving in the Philippines, and one in Hawaii. The cavalry continued to comprise about one-fifth of the total US Army. By 1916 each cavalry regiment was officially organized to consist of a headquarters, a headquarters troop, a supply troop, a machine-gun troop and 12 lettered troops organized into three squadrons of four troops each. Until then, the trooper's life continued to be unmarred by excessive activity, with a few exceptions. During the San Francisco earthquake and fire of 1906, two cavalry regiments under the famous cavalryman and Arctic explorer General Adolphus Washington Greely, commander of all the armed forces on the scene, rushed in to preserve order and aid survivors. In the same year, a three-year intervention in Cuba began, during which two

The Philippine Islands would prove to be a costly acquisition as the twentieth century unfolded. In 1898, when US soldiers first landed on the islands, few Americans had ever heard of them.

cavalry regiments formed part of the occupying force. In 1916 the 11th and 12th Cavalry were sent in to restore order in the Colorado mine fields, where there was serious labor trouble involving the famous labor leader Mother Jones. During their stay of nine months, the troopers encountered no difficulties. The next real fighting the cavalry saw began somewhat farther south, in the little border town of Columbus, New Mexico.

At about four o'clock in the morning of 9 March 1916, Mexican bandit-patriot Pancho Villa hit Columbus, New Mexico, which was garrisoned at the time by the 13th Cavalry, with a force of up to 1500 men. Leader of a violently anti-American faction popular in northern Mexico, Robin Hood to many, General Francisco (Pancho) Villa, whose real name was Doroteo Arango, neither smoked nor drank; his critics claimed he was too busy murdering, raping and looting. Villa's raid on Columbus had little military significance, although it greatly enhanced his prestige. It was probably motivated by his anger at the United States for its recognition of his arch-rival Don Venustiano Carranza as *de facto* head of the Mexican government.

Among those attacking Columbus at dawn were undoubtedly Villa's elite 300-man bodyguard, known as *Dorados* because of the gold insignia they wore on their olive uniforms and Stetsons. Mostly Yaqui Indians, each an excellent marksman and superbly mounted, the *Dorados* carried Winchester rifles and two sidearms. Unencumbered by families or camp followers, they were the most mobile of Villa's men, responsible for many of his boldest coups.

Villa's men killed sentries, but they did not enter Columbus without detection. While troopers of the 13th tumbled out of bed – only four troops of the regiment were in town, as the regimental polo team had just returned from a match at Fort Bliss – the *Villistas* rode up and down Broadway, Columbus's main street, smashing, looting and burning. While the dismounted troopers were being rapidly assembled by their officers, the raiders committed what proved to be a tactical error by setting fire to the Commercial Hotel, illuminating themselves for Lieutenant Lucas, commander of the machine-gun platoon, who was having his men set up one of the guns. It jammed. Lucas deployed his remaining guns and troopers as dismounted rifles, posting them so that the *Villistas* were between them and the burning hotel, and opened fire at the perfectly silhouetted Mexicans. Their withering fire took a heavy toll. At the western end of town, where the attack began, the raiders had dragged officers and civilians from their homes or chased them into the mesquite. Several kitchen crews, surrounded in their mess shacks, defended themselves with the shotguns kept on hand to kill quail and rabbits. In one shack the crew used a pot of boiling water, axes and a baseball bat

and actually killed a few of the raiders. It had been a costly raid for Villa. Sixty-seven dead Mexicans were found and burned the next day. American losses totaled seven troopers killed, five wounded; eight civilians killed and two wounded.

As the *Villistas* withdrew, the troopers finally had time to get to their horses. Major Frank Tompkins gathered a mounted detachment of 32 men and pursued the *Villistas* to about 15 miles below the border, sniping stragglers and rearguardsmen with their sidearms, stopping only when their horses played out. Tompkins's

Top: *US troops with casualties of a fight at Mount Dajo, Jolo, Philippines, during the insurrection of 1908–09.*

Above: *Cavalry played a decreasing role in frontal-assault actions from the Napoleonic Wars to the late nineteenth century, while infantrymen increasingly dominated combat as a result of new weapons and technology.*

even for the peace-seeking Wilson Administration. The day after the raid, President Wilson ordered a Punitive Expedition into Mexico to bring Villa back dead or alive. Wilson, although he had never had a real grasp of Mexican politics, backed Carranza. But like the rest of official America, his administration was much more concerned with the growing war in Europe, particularly deteriorating US relations with Germany, than with the volatile situation south of the border. While at first Carranza appeared to accept America's assistance in chastising his arch-rival (at the time Villa had Carranza more or less besieged in Mexico City), it soon became clear that expecting *Carranzistas* to support an American expeditionary force in Mexico was like expecting Democrats in America to support Mexican invaders gunning for Republicans. Failing to understand that Carranza was only slightly less violently anti-American than Villa, Wilson insisted that the Punitive Expedition proceed with 'scrupulous regard for the sovereignty of Mexico,' and placed so many restrictions on it that the expedition was effectively hampered from the outset. Troopers were forbidden to carry their rifles; their Colt .45 Automatics were their only weapons. Brigadier General John J 'Black Jack' Pershing, chosen to lead the expedition, was forbidden to use the railroads, to enter Mexican towns, or to use the telegraph lines without permission of the Carranza Government, which was almost never granted. Eventually, there was almost as much fighting between the expedition and the *Carranzistas* as between the expedition and the *Villistas*.

Pershing's force of about 5000 troops crossed the border on 15 March 1916, less than one week after Villa rode out of Columbus. Despite the famous photograph of Pershing on horseback leading his mounted headquarters party out of the Santa Maria River, Pershing's mount of choice for the expedition was a black Dodge touring car. Three other Dodges filled with war correspondents and the general's escort followed behind. But the Punitive Expedition was primarily a cavalry expedition with supporting infantry, artillery and various service detachments, including at various times all or parts of the 5th, 6th, 7th, 10th, 11th, 12th and 13th Cavalry. Eight airplanes of the 13 that constituted the entire US Air Force of the day (the 1st Aero Squadron of the Signal Corps, all Curtis JN-2s or 'Jennies') with their 10 officers and 82 men, also joined the expedition. This was their first appearance in a campaign by the US Army; they were primarily used to carry messages. Unfortunately, the planes soon cracked up in the rough Mexican countryside, where replacements and repairs were impossible. Far more notable in their failure on the expedition were the trucks, which also came to grief in the Mexican terrain. Their introduction into the logistics system was a major innovation, and although their mechanical failures occasioned

Mexican insurrectionist Pancho Villa on the march with his soldiers during the Mexican Civil War.

report estimated that at least another 75-100 raiders were killed by his harassing tactics, bringing total Mexican losses in the raid to nearly 200.

America was outraged. The town of Humboldt, Iowa, put up a $10,000 reward for Villa, dead or alive. Colonel Herbert Slocum, commander of the 13th Cavalry, put up a $50,000 reward from his own money, and George M Cohan wrote a song. The attack was too much

many inconveniences, valuable lessons were learned. Old-fashioned horse- and mule-drawn wagons remained the chief means of supply.

One of General Pershing's aides on the expedition was First Lieutenant George S Patton, Jr, on special service with the command. Known later by his men in Sicily and North Africa as 'Pistol-Packing Patton' because of the pearl-handled revolvers he always wore (he was also known as 'Old Blood and Guts'), one incident in particular demonstrated his ability to use them. While on a foraging mission with seven men in three automobiles, Patton approached a large farm house known to belong to one of Villa's colonels. Patton, believing the colonel might be at home, posted his men at all the exits, covering the front gate to the courtyard himself. Suddenly three horsemen armed with rifles and pistols galloped out of the front gate straight at him. Constrained by the restrictions of the expedition to hold fire until hostile identification was certain, Patton waited until the men fired at him, then killed all three with his pistols. One of the dead horsemen proved to be Villa's colonel.

Pershing split his command into two columns, leading the west column south from Columbus himself. With him went the black 10th Cavalry, the unit he had captained in Cuba; the 7th, an infantry regiment; and a battery of the 6th Field Artillery with three-inch field-pieces. Also with Pershing were the 13th Cavalry with two infantry regiments and another battery of the 6th Field Artillery. The rest of the army moved down on the border, leaving the coast artillery to protect the seaboard. President Wilson federalized 75,000 National Guardsmen in May and sent them to join the Regulars on the border. Their number was doubled in June.

Twelve days after crossing the border, the Punitive Expedition set up headquarters at Colonia Dublan near the Casas Grandes River, 125 miles south of Columbus in the Mexican state of Chihuahua. Up to that point, Villa had stayed close to the river, and his trail had been easy to follow, but here he split up his army into several units. Pershing sent swift columns of the 7th, 10th, 11th and 13th Cavalry south into the desert and mountain vastness with orders to find Villa and bring him back dead or alive. Cut off from any base, these columns had to live off the land in the way of the old cavalry of the Indian wars: it was, in fact, the last campaign of the old US Cavalry. Each horse carried about 250 pounds through the heat, wind and dust of the Chihuahua desert, shivering at night in the high-altitude cold. Quite likely, Villa's forces hid in the little towns the expedition was forbidden to enter. During his first press conference, held at Colonia Dublan, when asked how long it would take to get Villa, one of Pershing's scouts replied that they had Villa completely surrounded – on one side. The General said the campaign might be just beginning.

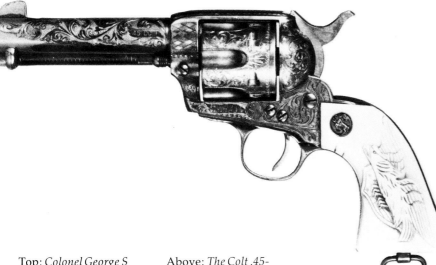

Top: *Colonel George S Patton, Jr, commanded the 5th Cavalry during the second half of 1938 and was a lifelong advocate of the cavalry role in modern warfare.*

Above: *The Colt .45-caliber automatic pistol became standard issue in 1911. General Patton habitually wore a pair of these weaspons, earning the nickname 'Pistol Packing Patton.'*

On 29 March, at seven o'clock in the morning, after a 17-hour march through freezing weather over a precipitous mountain range, 400 horsemen of Colonel George A Dodd's 7th Cavalry made contact with Villa and 500 of his men at Guerrero, west of Chihuahua City. This would be the only battle of the expedition directly involving the rebel leader. The *Villistas* fired first, and the 7th Cavalry responded, killing 60 – including the commanding officer – and wounding many others before the Mexicans fled. Dodd followed Villa until his army evaporated into cities and areas the expedition was forbidden to enter. Dodd was certain he could have cut off escape routes and taken Villa if he had arrived at Guerrero a few hours earlier.

Pershing had now penetrated 270 miles south of Columbus, and learned that Crook's methods of using local informants and native scouts in the Indian wars would not work in Mexico. Mexicans of all tribes and castes considered Villa and his Yaquis patriots, and sheltered them from the invading *norteamericanos*; informants often led the troopers on circuitous routes that gave the *Villistas* plenty of time to escape. Nevertheless, on 10 April Major Frank Tompkins with two troops of the 13th Cavalry trailed Villa into the city of Parral, about 150 miles south of Chihuahua City. At Parral he was invited in by the *Carranzista* General Ismael Lozano to refresh himself and his troops. Smelling a trap, Tompkins got his men out of town quickly under the leveled guns of the *Carranzista* garrison. Once outside the city where he had been advised to camp, he was attacked by a superior force of *Carranzistas* who pursued him for 15 miles and forced him to retreat north. On the journey his rearguard killed at least 40 of their attackers. There was no longer any question that the whole countryside opposed the invading *gringos*. Pershing asked for and got more troops, but even with civilian truck convoys beginning to work, without trains it was nearly impossible to supply them. Villa broke his command into small bands and scattered them all over the country. Pershing did the same, organizing his command into five separate and autonomous districts, despairing of receiving any accurate information from native informants: 'I have the honor to inform you that according to all information that is true and verified, Villa is at this moment in all parts and none in particular.'

Even so, the cavalry continued to engage roving bands of *Villistas*, and Major Robert L Howze devastated the bands of two of Villa's lieutenants, Acosta and Dominguez. By June there were US Army troops all over Mexico. News reached Pershing that Villa had been killed in a battle with *Carranzistas*; American intelligence concluded that Carranza was determined to force Pershing's expedition out of Mexico. Carranza himself said Villa was dead, and that the *Yanquis* had no more business in Mexico. Other rumors claimed that Villa was armed by Germany. With Mexican troops reported moving into the Parral area, Pershing requested another cavalry regiment, and expansion of all units to maximum strength. But a rumor reached Washington that Germany was backing Carranza, and that he had agreed to move his army between Pershing and the border to prevent the US Regular Army from participating in the war in Europe.

Left: *General John J Pershing (left) with staff members of the 10th Cavalry during the Punitive Expedition into Mexico in 1916.*

Right: *Pershing's pursuit of Pancho Villa in 1916 was hamstrung by numerous restrictions placed upon him by President Woodrow Wilson. At the time, Wilson was more concerned about the protracted war in Europe than about the Mexican Revolution.*

In June, when hope of catching Villa had been effectively abandoned, Carranza's commander of the North advised Pershing to go home, informing him that Mexico would not permit him to move American soldiers west, south, or east. Shortly thereafter, at a time when Pershing had already consolidated his forces at Colonia Dublan – and the principal activity of the cavalry had become polo – a large force of *Carranzistas* opened fire on two troops of the 10th Cavalry whose commander foolishly led them through the town of Carrizal. Two officers and ten men were killed, 11 wounded, and 23 troopers taken prisoner. At this point President Wilson called in most of the remaining National Guardsmen to police the border, and war probably would have broken out then and there but for the bitter struggle raging in Europe. Anxious not to become embroiled in a war with Mexico at a time when war with Germany was a growing possibility, Wilson agreed to submit the disputes stemming from the expedition to a joint commission for settlement. In January 1917, as relations between the United States and Germany reached the critical stage, the expedition was withdrawn. The last unit of the last cavalry expedition of the US Cavalry crossed the border at 3:00 PM on Monday, 5 February 1917.

Although Pershing failed to capture Villa, he probably would have if the *Carranzistas* had co-operated, or if the cavalry had been allowed a free hand. In any case, both Villa and Carranza were assassinated within the next year. The dispersal of Villa's band and the strengthening of border forces put an end to serious border incidents. More important, from a military point of view, not since the Civil War had a sizable

Top: *US Cavalry training remained much the same as it had been in the nineteenth century almost until World War II.*

Above: *Saber practice combined with jumping.*

Opposite: *Both horse and rider seem doubtful that they can negotiate the steep incline successfully in this equestrian-training photo from the early 1920s.*

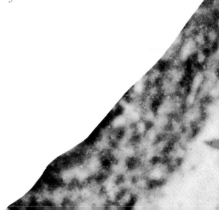

American force been assembled for a sufficient period to train officers in the field grade. New logistic systems and new technologies – notably the gasoline engine – were tested, as were the old. Pershing wrote, 'This Expedition has been a great thing for the Cavalry, as it has demonstrated beyond question the necessity for this arm for the future service of this kind.' His opinion was respected in the passage of much-needed legislation affecting national defense, in which a significant increase in cavalry was authorized, and many defects in the military establishment were uncovered in time to be corrected before the Army was thrown into the cauldron of war in Europe.

The Metamorphosis of the US Cavalry

Previous pages: *The cavalry became airmobile just in time to play a key role in the war in Vietnam.*

Below: *A US Cavalry recruiting poster of 1920.*

On 3 June 1916, while Pershing's cavalrymen were still pursuing Villa in Mexico, Congress passed the National Defense Act and established a coherent military policy at last. The long-overdue act supplanted a host of expedient measures. Ten regiments were scheduled to be added to the cavalry over a period of five years, creating two permanent divisions, each consisting of a headquarters, three brigades (of three cavalry regiments each), a horse field-artillery regiment, a mounted engineer battalion, a mounted signal battalion, an aero squadron, and the concomitant ammunition, supply, engineer and sanitary trains. The remaining ten cavalry regiments were assigned one each to the seven newly authorized infantry divisions, to perform reconnaissance and security missions. By the time America entered World War I, two of the new regiments authorized by the National Defense Act had been organized (the 16th and the 17th), bringing total American cavalry strength at the declaration of war on Germany to 17 regiments. But there were clear signals that the startling effectiveness of modern infantry and artillery weapons was restricting cavalry to a secondary role. One

Opposite, top: *Cavalrymen of the interwar period taking an obstacle course.*

THE HORSE IS MAN'S NOBLEST COMPANION

HORST SCHRECK.
1920.

JOIN THE

CAVALRY

and have a courageous friend

U.S. ARMY RECRUITING OFFICE:

month after the next new cavalry regiments were organized, the 18th through the 25th began training as field artillery; on 1 November 1917 all eight were permanently redesignated as the 76th through the 83rd Field Artillery.

Despite pronounced sympathies – America was, after all, a people made up chiefly from those nations at war – there had at first been little American desire to take part in the war in Europe. But President Wilson's determination to remain 'impartial in thought as well as in action' slowly weakened under the pressure of German U-boat predations, and early in 1917 the United States severed diplomatic relations with Germany. The publication in March of an intercepted German message to Mexico, proposing an alliance between Germany and Mexico if the United States entered the war, pushed America closer to the brink. Wilson announced that American merchant marine ships would be armed for self-defense. German U-boats promptly sank several US merchantmen in quick succession – claiming American lives – and two months and one day after Pershing withdrew the Punitive Expedition from Mexico, President Wilson signed a joint Congressional

resolution plunging the United States into war with Germany.

All but one of America's Regular Cavalry regiments were to remain on the Mexican border for the duration of the war. Although only the 2nd United States Cavalry (without their troop horses) went to France, the cavalry lived up to its of leadership role by supplying Major General John J Pershing, America's best-known general, to direct the entire 4,000,000-man American Expeditionary Force (AEF). The principal task of the 2nd Cavalry in France was to man numerous remount stations devoted to caring for mules and horses used for transport. The automobile, the truck, barbed wire and new weapons had revolutionized warfare; the trench and the machine gun made combat use of the horse impractical. Without mobility, there was little place for cavalry, and where there was, cavalry's traditional functions were challenged by tanks and airplanes. If the experiences of the Western Front proved anything of military significance, it was that armor was infinitely superior to horsemen. As one American observer pointed out, infantry could make themselves invisible on the battlefield by throwing themselves flat on

Above: *Brigadier General Maxwell Murray and Colonel George S Patton, Jr. review the 16th FA before the United States entered World War II.*

the ground, but horses were exterminated. 'You can't make a cavalry charge until you have captured the enemy's last machine gun.'

Although great masses of European cavalry set out on raids in the first days of the war – ten German divisions (70,000) faced ten French cavalry divisions and one British in France – there were no important cavalry victories on the Western Front. European cavalrymen were armed with lances and sabers. Under the new battle conditions, the French soon split their force into useless detachments; the Germans were quickest of all to abandon their horses. Theoretically, the function of cavalry on the Western Front was to gallop through the breach made by the victorious infantry – through the 'G' in 'Gap' – turning the enemy's defeat into a rout. But no such gap appeared. Lloyd George, visiting France in 1916, recalled, 'When I ventured to express my doubts as to whether cavalry could ever operate successfully on a front bristling for miles behind the enemy's lines with barbed wire and machine guns . . . the Generals fell on me.' A French officer remarked facetiously, 'You know there's nothing like a lance against machine guns.'

On the Eastern Front, Russia entered the war with 24 cavalry divisions (200,000 horsemen), only to scatter and weaken the potential of this force by spreading it along its entire frontier. Russia in fact suffered its most crushing defeat of the war when a single German cavalry division succeeded in delaying the arrival of Rennenkampf's army at Tannenberg. Russia

later increased its cavalry to 54 divisions, a force so ponderous it contributed greatly to the breakdown of the Russian transportation system. Under British General Edmund Allenby in Palestine, cavalry achievements in the war reached their highest plane when Allenby defeated a strong Turkish army at Megiddo by exploiting cavalry's mobility. Even so, a great deal of his success must be credited to the supporting role of bombardment aviation.

A small portion of US Cavalry finally did see mounted action in France, late in August 1918 when the Germans were greatly weakened and a war of movement appeared possible. Fourteen officers and 404 men from troops B, D, F and H of the 2nd Cavalry, mounted on convalescent horses from the veterinary hospital, formed a provisional squadron and rode out to take part in the September offensive of the Allies. One of its troop commanders was Captain E N Harmon, who later, as General Harmon, won distinction in World War II as an armored commander. The troopers were used for liaison, reconnaissance and pursuit of retreating Germans, a few of whom they captured, until they were withdrawn from the front in mid-October with only 150 mounts still serviceable.

Despite the small part played by cavalry on the Western Front, and its general lack of effectiveness everywhere, all the great generals involved in the conflict, including Germany's Erich von Ludendorff, were emphatic in their belief that cavalry remained an essential arm of service. As expressed by General Pershing, who as leader of

US Cavalry passing through St Baussant on 12 September 1918 – one of the few American mounted units to see action in France.

the recent Punitive Expedition was the only
Allied general to have experienced trench warfare and a campaign of movement within the
same year, 'There is not in the world today an
officer of distinction, recognized as an authority
on military matters in a broad way, who does not
declare with emphasis that cavalry is as important today as it ever has been.' Meanwhile,
Pershing was sufficiently impressed by the
prospects of armored mounts to request 600
heavy and 1200 light tanks to be produced in the
United States (none reached France in time to
see action). In fact, the vanquished von Ludendorff described the Allied tanks as a principal
factor in Germany's defeat. Although the tank of
World War I was slow, clumsy, unwieldy,
difficult to control and mechanically unreliable,
it had proved its value in combat, and the
writing was on the wall. But few leaders on
either side realized how totally armor and the
internal-combustion engine would restore
shock and mobility to combat and revolutionize
warfare.

Tanks originated from a suggestion by
English officer Lieutenant-Colonel Ernest D
Swinton, who saw American-made caterpillar
tractors with tracks in France in 1914 and
thought they might be armored and armed for
combat. His idea was supported by First Lord of
the Admiralty Winston S Churchill and deve-

Top: *During World War I,
it became clear that
armored 'mounts' would
have to assume the role
previously played by the
horse in the new age of
total warfare.*

Left: *On the Eastern Front,
Russia fielded a total of 24
cavalry divisions (200,000
men) early in World War I;
this number more than
doubled during the conflict.*

171

Mounted troopers with supply horses on a field exercise during the last days of the horse cavalry.

loped as a type of 'land ship' by the Royal Navy. Hence such nautical tank terms as hatch, hull, bow and ports. Developed under top secrecy, the first models shipped to France were labeled *tanks* – for use as water tanks by Russia – and the name stuck. The tank first saw action in the Somme area on 15 September 1916. From the outset, the tank was thought of as an auxiliary to and part of the infantry, which was to exploit holes made by tanks in enemy lines. Its potential value was understood by few on either side during the war; the Germans produced only a few late in the conflict. Of a total of 90 tanks fielded by Germany in 1918, 75 had been captured from the Allies. The first American tank units to see action (12 September 1918) were elements of the 304th Tank Brigade using French Renault light tanks, commanded by cavalryman Lieutenant-Colonel George S Patton, who still wore his six-shooters. The American Tank Corps supported infantry in most actions, but also executed normal cavalry reconnaissance missions. Combined tank-horse cavalry actions, such as that attempted by the British at Amiens on 1 August 1918, proved to be of dubious success. 'When there was no fire, the cavalry outstripped these tanks, and as soon as fire was opened the cavalry were unable to follow the tanks. Tied down to support the cavalry, [the tanks] were a long way behind the infantry advance . . . as cavalry cannot make themselves invisible on the battlefield by throwing themselves flat on the ground.'

Above: *Tenth Cavalry troopers of the 1930s, when they were still commanded by white officers. Discrimination remained endemic in the military until after World War II.*

Left: *Camp Funston, Kansas, was the scene of this 2nd Cavalry practice problem in negotiating swampy terrain (1942).*

After the war, the American desire for demobilization led to a drastic cut in cavalry strength. The National Defense Act of 1920 established the office of Chief of Cavalry (first filled by Major General Willard A Holbrook). But by 1921 the number of cavalry regiments had been reduced from 17 to 14 and mounted-arm personnel had been cut by more than one-half, as squadrons and troops of the remaining regiments were placed on an inactive status. The 1st Cavalry Division, retained as a unit, was trimmed to the absolute minimum in head-quarters, and to two brigades of two lean regiments each, a battalion of horse artillery, a mounted engineer battalion and an ambulance company. Officers of the Regular Cavalry without regimental assignments were employed to train National Guard and Cavalry Reserve units. By mid-1923 the Regular Cavalry totaled 721 officers and 8887 men, these numbers remaining relatively constant until the late 1930s. Between the wars, progress in equitation interrupted by World War I was resumed, and a great deal of polo was played. On more than one occasion, American cavalrymen took highest honors in international competition.

Despite the lessons of World War I, the cavalry was slow in adopting mechanization. Staunch cavalrymen insisted that the stalemate on the Western Front in World War I was the exception, and the AEF Cavalry Board concluded, 'The role of cavalry, in general, has changed but little

173

An early mechanized-cavalry reconnaissance trooper during field exercises at Fort Riley, Kansas, site of the US Cavalry Museum.

when considering war of movement.' Progress in the motor-vehicle industry and in the design of armor and armament, and the abundance of oil in the United States notwithstanding, only a few light mechanized vehicles were being used by the cavalry during the 1920s. In 1928, at the urging of Secretary of War Dwight D Davis, the army began a series of experiments to develop tank and mechanized forces. Trucks and automobiles were finally added to replace the cavalry's wagons and pack animals. It was not until the 1930s that the mechanized cavalry regiment, equipped with combat cars, became a reality. As late as 1938, Chief of Cavalry Major General John K Herr, who favored a balanced force of both horses and mechanized cavalry, was able to assert, 'We must not be misled to our own detriment to assume that the untried machine can displace the proved and tried horse.'

The first great step toward mechanization occurred in 1931, when Army Chief of Staff General Douglas MacArthur directed all arms and services to adopt mechanization and motorization to the greatest extent needed to execute their missions. The cavalry, in particular, was urged to develop combat vehicles that would 'enhance its power in roles of reconnaissance, counterreconnaissance, flank action, pursuit and similar operations.' Two years later the other shoe fell. In MacArthur's words, 'The

horse has no higher degree of mobility today then he had a thousand years ago. The time has therefore arrived when the Cavalry arm must either replace or assist the horse as a means of transportation, or else pass into the limbo of discarded military formations.' In January 1933 the first American mechanized cavalry organization came into being, when the 1st Cavalry dismounted and began to replace horses with machines at Fort Knox, Kentucky, where the cavalry had chosen to develop and test combat vehicles. Over the next four years, a battalion of field artillery, a quartermaster company, the 13th Cavalry and other units moved to Fort Knox and mechanized. They were combined in 1938 to form the first mechanized cavalry brigade under Brigadier General Daniel Van Voorhis, the 7th Cavalry Brigade (Mechanized). Van Voorhis was soon succeeded by Colonel Adna R Chaffee, well-known pioneer of mechanization, whose dedication to the development of armor at Fort Knox and on the War Department General Staff earned him the title 'Father of the Armored Force.'

The distinctive characteristics of mechanized cavalry were to be great mobility, armor protection and firepower; its principal role was 'in employment on distant missions covering a wide area,' although it was not expected to hold objectives for any length of time without artillery and infantry or horse-cavalry support.

Similar in organization to the horse regiment, the mechanized regiment of 1932 consisted of 42 officers and 610 enlisted men, divided into a covering squadron, a combat-car squadron, a machine-gun troop and a headquarters troop. Its four lettered troops were equipped with combat

Right: *Standard bearer of G Troop, 10th Cavalry, at Fort Riley in 1942.*

Above: *Mounted troopers lead a pack horse carrying a machine gun during World War II.*

vehicles instead of horses. The regiment's 35 combat cars (light, fast tanks called 'combat cars' chiefly to distinguish them from the light tanks of the infantry), were divided among the two troops of the combat-car squadron and one troop of the covering squadron; the other covering squadron troop employed armored cars. To the mechanized division were added an armored-car troop, a tank company and an air observation squadron. The division had a war strength of 465 officers and 8840 men; it retained two brigades of horse soldiers.

An interesting experiment which combined the advantages of mechanization and horse cavalry saw the 4th and 6th regiments transformed into Horse-Mechanized Corps Reconnaissance Regiments (HMCRR). A squad of eight riders and horses with forage, rations and complete equipment, including heavy and light machine guns, could be loaded into a truck and trailer in five to seven minutes. As long as good roads were available, the troopers used fast motor transportation. When road conditions limited the efficiency of trucks, or when it became necessary to reconnoiter laterally off to the sides of the road itself, the troopers unloaded and mounted up. The experiment was such a success that most of the remaining National Guard cavalry regiments were transformed into seven HMCRR regiments, but the necessary equipment for the conversion was not delivered until late in 1941, and by then there was no opportunity to measure its effectiveness in maneuvers before Pearl Harbor.

In 1940 the total US Cavalry consisted of 12 regiments, two of which were HMCRR, and the

Above: *Tanks of the 77th Division on Leyte Island, 1945. The Philippines were the scene of the last action by a horse-cavalry unit in modern American warfare.*

Below: *General Jonathan Wainwright (here greeted by General Douglas MacArthur upon his return from a Japanese POW camp) commanded the 26th Cavalry on Bataan. The hard-pressed unit held out for three weeks after fodder for their horses ran out and the animals had to be killed – and eaten.*

26th Cavalry, the Philippine Scouts. The success of the German *blitzkrieg* in Poland in 1939 had dramatically demonstrated the speed and power of German armor, and profoundly affected military tactics and doctrine around the world. In America, advocates of the formation of true armored divisions could no longer be denied, and on 10 July 1940 an Armored Force was created around the nucleus of the 7th Cavalry Brigade (Mechanized), which merged with the Provisional Tank Brigade and the 6th Infantry (Armored) and was lost to the cavalry forever. The total demise of the horse was not to be far behind.

Mounted American Cavalry made its last appearance in strength during maneuvers with experimental armored forces in Louisiana late in 1940. Despite restrictions which prevented the cavalry from operating in its usual forward area and forced it to wait for the mechanized forces to move first, the 1st Cavalry Division astounded critics with quick cross-country marches, river fordings and decisive attacks. Although the mechanized forces dominated the maneuvers, the cavalrymen felt that their success under adverse artificial conditions indicated that had they been permitted to operate as if under real battle conditions, they would have silenced the critics of the horse forever.

On 7 December 1941, the Japanese bombed Pearl Harbor and the United States entered World War II. The rush to mechanization continued, but between December 1941 and April 1942 the 26th Cavalry – the Philippine Scouts – engaged in a series of tough and dramatic battles. Early in January the Japanese took Manila, and the 26th Cavalry covered the withdrawal of American forces to the Bataan Peninsula. As long as Bataan and Corregidor Island held out, the Japanese would be unable to use Manila Harbor. The 26th Cavalry managed to secure a defensible position on Bataan, but the only fodder available for the horses was rice

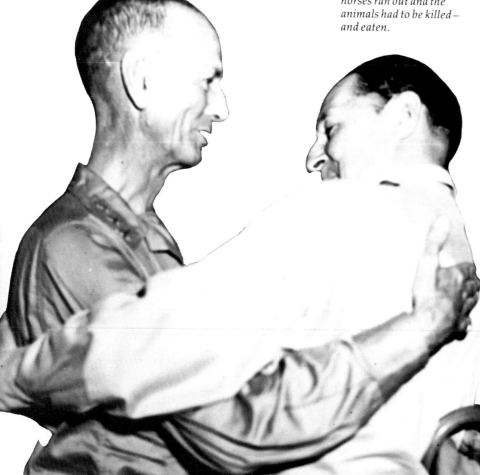

straw from the last harvest. After a few weeks of fierce fighting, rations for the men were reduced to 200 grams of rice a day. On 12 March, when General Johnathan Wainwright took command, hunger, heat, malaria, dysentery and casualties had made life unbearable. The Japanese were advancing in force again, and the horses had eaten all the rice straw on Bataan.

On 15 March 1942, the last horses of a Regular American Army unit to see action met their end in the stew pot; 250 horses and 48 mules were slaughtered and eaten. 'Their tough flesh tasted good with curry and rice,' a hungry soldier reported. Dismounted, the 26th fought on. Among the 2000 survivors in the final disorderly escape from Bataan on the night of 8 April were three or four troopers, all that was left of the courageous regiment. Citing the heroism and skill of the 26th, General Wainwright, as the last senior American officer to employ cavalry against an armed enemy, suggested that the mounted cavalry still had a place in the United States Army.

His pleas fell on deaf ears. In March 1942 the War Department eliminated the office of Chief of Cavalry, along with the chiefs of the other combat arms, and the horse cavalry was effectively abolished. The trend toward mechanization accelerated. The 1st Cavalry Division was dismounted and trained for jungle fighting in the Pacific Theater, where it fought as a unit in four major campaigns and performed occupational duties in Japan after the war. Generals MacArthur and Kreuger called it the best division in their commands; Secretary of War Patterson called it the best in the world. Not only did the 1st Cavalry Division keep its name, but its companies continued to be called 'troops' and its men 'troopers.' Wearing the yellow cavalry insignia, the troopers marched under the red and white guidons of the old horse regiment; the division artillerymen wore red scarfs in parade, but the troopers continued to wear yellow.

Above: *A tank destroyer attached to the 5th US Army in Italy; the cavalry used lighter tanks, largely for reconnaissance rather than combat.*

Left: *The tank has played an increasing part in modern warfare since its introduction in 1916.*

Main picture: *US M-3 tanks advance to strengthen Allied positions at the Kasserine Pass, Tunisia, 1943.*
Right: *The speed and scope of General Patton's operations in North Africa, Sicily and Europe testified to his cavalry experience.*

The remaining mounted regiments were transformed into armored and mechanized units; most of the 73 nondivisional cavalry units active during the war were mechanized reconnaissance units attached to armored and infantry divisions – although purely reconnaissance missions were rare, and combat roles more common. By the end of the war, total cavalry strength reached 91,948. In the sweeps through North Africa, Sicily, Italy, and Belgium, and the final Allied drive across Europe, mechanized forces functioned in the traditional cavalry role. Armor, as the ground-mobility arm functioning like cavalry, emerged from World War II with a large share of credit for the Allied victory, and cavalry's postwar role was envisioned as an amplification of its traditional role, using mechanization and armor. General George S Patton's breathtaking sweeps through North Africa and Sicily, and later through Europe, were nothing if not cavalry maneuvers, and Patton, with his pistols on his hips, was nothing if not a cavalryman who understood that some of the mounts had changed. His high-speed, high-powered 6th Cavalry Group Army Information Service – popularly known as Patton's Household Cavalry – performed like a reincarnation of Jeb Stuart in supplying information necessary for the success of the final Allied drive in Europe.

Right: *Members of the 3rd Armored Division bypass a disabled German tank en route to Langlir, Belgium, early in 1945.*

While no horses went overseas in World War II, troopers drilled on horseback daily until they shipped out, and saber charges were practiced. Requests for horse cavalry arrived throughout the war from field commanders who knew best the conditions under which they were fighting, and after the war General Patton joined many who believed that the mounted trooper had not outlived his usefulness, adding, 'Had we possessed an American cavalry division with pack artillery in Tunisia and Sicily not a German would have escaped.' Nor did the military use of horses end with the demise of the 26th Cavalry in the Philippines. In the jungles of Burma and India, a unit under Brigadier General Frank D Merrill, nicknamed 'Merrill's Marauders,' used approximately 340 horses and 360 mules. In Sicily, the 3rd Infantry Division organized the Provisional Reconnaissance Troop, Mounted, which served in the mountains during the invasion of Italy and included 143 horses and 349 mules in September 1943.

Great numbers of horses were used by the European powers in World War II: 2,750,000 – twice as many as in World War I – served Germany, for both cavalry and transport; 3,500,000 served Russia. It is estimated that 865 horses died every day for the German Reich; 52,000 horses died in the siege of Stalingrad. The

Above: *World War II armor, providing the ground mobility previously furnished by the horse, contributed to the Allied victory in all theaters.*

Above: *During World War II, Allied forces learned how to combine armor and infantry effectively: here an American soldier trains his machine gun down a French street.*

Top: *The Germans used both tanks, like this ruined MK 4, and horses in World War II; well over 2 million cavalry and transport horses served the Reich.*

Polish Cavalry, which actually faced *Panzers* with lancers, suffered 90 percent casualties. Never before had horses been used so recklessly. Especially on the Russian Front, they played an important role, operating with devastating effect behind enemy lines in 30°-below-zero weather, stemming the tide until the Soviets rebuilt their armored formations. Germany disbanded its horse cavalry for a time, but turned to it again toward the end of the war. When the Reich's 17th Army evacuated the Crimea in 1944, tens of thousands of horses were machine-gunned and tossed into the sea to prevent them from falling into Russian hands.

After the war America demobilized rapidly. Except for a few ceremonial mounts, the War Department sold all the cavalry horses, equipment and posts. The horse cavalry was extinguished, but, in general, the names, traditions, missions and internal organization (squadrons and troops) of the old cavalry units passed to armored regiments and divisions and to mechanized reconnaissance units. The armored cavalry regiment of 1948 was equipped with 72 light and 69 medium tanks, for use by its three reconnaissance battalions, and had an authorized strength of 2883. After much controversy, the Army Organization Act of 1950 welded mechanized cavalry and armored units into a single armor branch. Curiously enough, while newspapers in the States were bewailing the passing of horse cavalry, 10 platoons of horsemen were on duty in Germany with the US Constabulary, a postwar peace-keeping force formed in 1946 from armored and cavalry units.

The 1st continued to be the only cavalry division as such, and all its units bore the traditional cavalry designations. The division

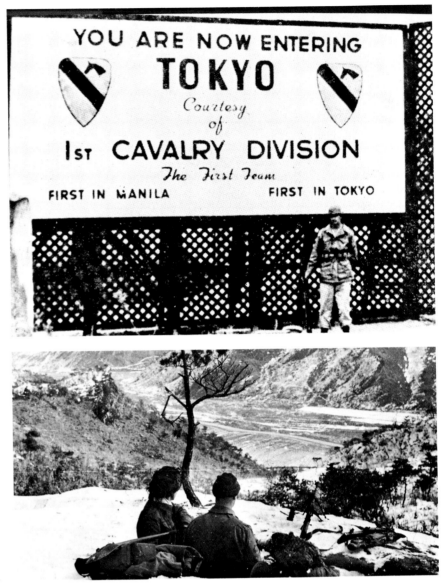

Top: *The 1st Cavalry proudly proclaimed itself 'First in Manila, First in Tokyo' in this 1945 billboard.*

Above: *Korea's forbidding terrain made the going rough for the 1st Cavalry Division when it joined UN forces in the field in July 1950.*

Left: *The Korean War was the first in which helicopters played a significant role as combat vehicles.*

was on occupational duty in Japan on 25 June 1950, when North Korea attacked South Korea in what was both a civil war between peoples of a divided country and an eruption of tensions between the two great power blocs that had emerged from World War II. US forces under General MacArthur, who soon became commander-in-chief of all UN forces, responded to the UN call for members to aid South Korea. The 1st Cavalry Division began arriving in Korea piecemeal, its first units reaching Taejon on 18 July 1950 to take up position on the right flank of the UN line and relieve the pressure on the 24th Infantry Division, which had been holding out for two weeks. The United States, following demobilization from World War II, was in poor shape to go to war, especially in Asia. What postwar planning there had been was for a global, European, nuclear war; to many, the development of rockets, guided missiles, recoilless and atomic weapons had already rendered the tank obsolete, and there were few mechanized mounts on hand. It was not until late in August that significant American armor reached Korea, but for the remainder of the war, tank units of battalion size and smaller were in most combat actions. Activation in 1951 of the 11th Armored Cavalry brought the total active regiments of this type (including the 2nd, 3rd, 6th and 14th) to five, but none served in the Far East. As described in 1951, the primary role of the armored cavalry regiment was 'to engage in security, light combat and reconnaissance missions. The regiment is not designed to engage in combat with hostile armor or strongly organized defenses.'

The 1st Cavalry Division continued to fight on the ground. On 1 November 1950, at Unsan, the 8th Cavalry Regiment, in its first engagement with Chinese troops, was surrounded and cut off; it lost approximately half its personnel, as well as hundreds of vehicles and artillery pieces. Fighting raged day and night, with Chinese and American soldiers wrestling each other to the ground, shooting from the hip and lobbing grenades at close range. The Chinese sometimes attacked in waves, blowing horns and whistles, firing Katusha rockets and mortar shells, their bodies piling up three deep. Between attacks, the Americans salvaged what weapons and ammunition they could from their dead enemies to use against the next wave. The Chinese took most of what was left of the entire third battalion with them when they withdrew north. 1st Cavalry Division tanks got their licks in later, in Chipyong-Wonju fighting in 1951, but one wonders if any of the cut-off, pinned-down

Above: *The Sheridan tank was named for the Union Cavalry leader who left his imprint on modern warfare.*

Top: *A US tank on the Korean Front fires from its .50-caliber machine gun.*

troopers at Unsan wished for their horses. Late in 1950, Red guerrilla cavalry decimated American forces retreating from the Yalu River; the rugged mountainous terrain of Korea often precluded ground mobility by wheel or track.

Two innovations of the Korean War were to have a pronounced effect upon American cavalry. Armored personnel carriers began to play an important role. Even more importantly, the Korean War was the first conflict in which helicopters saw useful service. The limited payloads of most types then available generally restricted their use to scouting and casualty-evacuation missions, but the US Marines' use of helicopters as combat vehicles during the first weeks of the war proved so successful that the Army, Navy and Air Force soon added them to their equipment arsenals.

After the Korean Armistice Agreement of 27 July 1953, America did not begin the immediate and drastic demobilization which had followed all its other wars. Winston Churchill later commented that the importance of the Korean War lay in the fact that it led to the rearming of America. By 1953 it was clear that future wars would depend on forces already in being when war started, and that the United States would never again have the luxury of being shielded by its allies while it mobilized its resources. Nuclear politics and permanent tensions between the two major global power blocs necessitated a permanent state of readiness; on the one hand, the felt need was for a vast nuclear arsenal and delivery system for retaliation and deterrence; on the other, conflicts like Korea, 'brush-fire' wars and flare-ups, as in Lebanon in

1958, pointed up the need for transportable ground forces. Between the Korean War and direct American involvement in Vietnam, defense reorganization at the highest levels (the Defense Reorganization Act of 1958 and ROAD, 1961) strengthened American ability to balance nuclear and conventional forces and to supply flexible command and control in operations with allies.

Among those units exemplifying the mobile in conventional forces was the 1st Cavalry Division (Airmobile), a force designed not to replace a standard infantry, armor, airborne or mechanical division, but to carry out a special kind of mobile military operation. It was one of the first US units to arrive in Vietnam after President Johnson approved a bill in 1965 committing ground forces to Southeast Asia in the struggle against communism. The 1st Squadron, 9th Cavalry (Air) arrived at An Khe in August, and by September the entire 16,000-man division, with over 400 aircraft (including over 300 helicopters) and 1600 vehicles, was ready to take up operations in the rugged central highlands. The same 1st Cavalry Division that fought throughout the Pacific and in Korea flew into the Ia Drang Valley in mid-November on mechanical mounts as part of Operation Silver Bayonet, and became the first American unit to engage a major North Vietnamese force for a prolonged fight, causing 1771 known enemy casualties. Vietnam was to be a helicopter war.

Main picture: *The combat helicopter has become increasingly sophisticated since the Korean War, as seen in this contemporary UH-60 Blackhawk participating in a training exercise at Fort Bragg, North Carolina.*

Opposite, top: *A trio of US Army helicopters widely used in Vietnam: top to bottom, UH-1B and UH-1D Iroquois and the AH-1G 'Huey.'*

Above: *The Armored Personnel Carrier (APC), first used extensively in Korea, came into its own in Vietnam for ground operations like this one by the 4th Cavalry near Saigon (1965).*

The helicopter, in its infancy in World War II, became the object of rapid development after Korea. The concept of 'Sky Cav,' in which helicopter cavalry was to operate in a strictly reconnaissance way, had existed in the mid-1950s, but it was obvious that helicopters could take troops, ordnance and artillery to and from battles in any terrain with a speed, mobility and accuracy never before possible. Development by Bell of the UH-1 Iroquois, which as the 'Huey' became the primary support helicopter in Vietnam, and by Boeing of the CH-47 Chinook, a heavy cargo helicopter capable of lifting divisional artillery, enabled the formation in January 1963 at Fort Benning, Georgia, of the 11th Air Assault Division. By the time it reached Vietnam in 1965, the 11th had metamorphosized into the reorganized 1st Cavalry Division (Airmobile). At about the same time, air cavalry troops with 26 helicopters each were assigned as part of the

The 'Sky Cav' concept has grown steadily since the mid-1950s to become an indispensable element of US Army planning and training; rapelling, as here, is an important skill for airborne troops.

armored cavalry squadron attached to every type of division.

Air cavalry in Vietnam functioned like the light horse of a century earlier. Acting on intelligence, a scout helicopter (usually a Hughes OH-6A Cayuse standard light observation helicopter, or 'Loach,' introduced in 1966) accompanied for protection by two AH-1G Huey gunship helicopters (a combination known as 'Pink Team'), flew at tree-top level or below, looking for signs of enemy activity – campsites, cooking fires, tracks. If the scout helicopter suspected enemy activity, an aerorifle platoon would be flown in by a UH-1D Huey to reconnoiter more thoroughly on the ground; a standby platoon was alerted and mounted their helicopters if the second platoon was called in by the aerorifle ground reconnaissance, enemy strength was deemed sufficient to warrant more support, and the responsibility passed from the

Top: *UH-1B gunship over Vietnam during Operation Pershing (May 1967).*

Above: *Air Assault School training at Fort Campbell, Kentucky.*

Above: *'Riding shotgun' in a Huey going into action in 1965.*

An M-113 APC of the 11th Armored Cavalry fights its way through dense undergrowth during a firefight at Long Binh, Vietnam: 23 February 1969.

air-cavalry troop to the brigade commander or division headquarters. Most likely, infantry or armored forces would be deployed. Once major forces arrived, the air cavalry was generally withdrawn; they were deemed too valuable to be used in a full-scale firefight. This routine, established by the 1st Squadron, 9th Cavalry (Air) at An Khe, was repeated daily throughout the war.

The success of the 1st Cavalry Division (Airmobile) in making swift responses to changing conditions, in fighting successive engagements at widely separated locales, in operating inside enemy territory and in providing ready backup to friendly forces expanded, by use of the helicopter, to all the Army's standard infantry units in Vietnam. Where once soldiers rode to battle on horseback, they now rode on helicopter; where once soldiers depended for ordnance and supplies on delivery by horse, they now depended on delivery by helicopter. At the beginning of 1965 the US Army had four light helicopter companies; by the end of June 1966, there were 45. Every major unit in every service arm in Vietnam, and in the South Vietnamese Army, had its own helicopter companies; the US Marines were by far the largest users of troop-carrying helicopters in Southeast Asia. But always in the vanguard, the flying horses of

airmobile cavalry, bearing crossed-saber emblems painted in yellow, kept alive the cavalry's unbroken tradition of shock and mobility, in operations code-named 'Pershing' and 'Jeb Stuart.'

Vietnam marked not only the coming of age of the helicopter, but the ascendancy of modern ground cavalry. The armored cavalry regiment of 1965 consisted of 132 tanks, a 48-helicopter air cavalry troop and 3349 men, but because US high command initially believed that the mountain and jungle terrain of Vietnam rendered armored operations impractical, it had to wait to provide its effectiveness. Except for a few US Marine tanks, the first American armored vehicles in Vietnam were created on the spot by divisional armor, which added extra machine guns and shields to M113 armored personnel carriers (APCs) to create a sort of light tank or reconnaissance vehicle known as the 'ACAV' (Armored Cavalry Assault Vehicle). The ACAV quickly proved that it could negotiate Vietnamese terrain, and added tactical flexibility to even the simplest encounter.

With approval finally won to try its tanks, armor in Vietnam made a major breakthrough in April 1966, when the 3rd Squadron, 4th Cavalry, with nine M48A3 tanks and 17 ACAVs, successfully escorted self-propelled 175mm guns and 8-inch howitzers through almost 100 miles of trackless jungle to fulfill a mission in support of the 1st Cavalry Division (Airmobile). Ground cavalry was then deployed in great numbers, and often worked closely with airborne infantry, holding the ambushing enemy in position until troops were lifted in by helicopter, then squeezing the enemy toward the infantry while supporting artillery cut off escape routes. Ground cavalry proved itself again in the face of the 1968 communist Tet Offensive, when together with US Marine and South Vietnamese armor it operated for 26 days in a densely populated area, and by moving quickly from one threatened sector to another, wore out the attackers. In a Vietcong offensive directed specifically at US troop concentrations and installations a few months later, mobile forces with the ability to maneuver rapidly and concentrate firepower drove the communist attackers back to the borders of South Vietnam.

US Cavalry won the battle, but it could not win the war. Nevertheless, it won survival of the service which for 200 years has been the vanguard of mobility for the US Army. As regards its methods, the only reasonable prediction that can be made is that change and progress will continue. Among other developments, the airborne tank – an object of experiment since World War II – is almost within the grasp of modern armor technology. But regardless of what shape the future takes, the horse, and the man on the horse, archetypal symbols of nobility and authority, continue to occupy a unique place in our consciousness. We have, after all, only to look at a chessboard to see who is ready to die for the king and queen. At the United States War College in Carlisle, Pennsylvania,

Top: *A 1st Cavalry Division leader and his Vietnamese interpreter on an intelligence-gathering mission in Thang Binh Province.*

Above: *Skytroopers of the 1st Cavalry (Airmobile) join Vietnamese National Police in checking out a village near Bong Son for signs of enemy presence (1967).*

Left: *Operation Junction City (1967) was the 11th Armored Cavalry's first major action in Vietnam. Here, members of the 1st squad repair mine damage to an APC.*

where our professional warriors maintain the traditions of honor, valor and patriotism, horsemanship is considered a personal virtue and a talisman of command. At the end of a global war he helped win largely through the skillful use of machines, the outspoken General George S Patton made it clear that he believed horse reconnaissance would always be necessary under certain circumstances; he also advocated the restoration of polo to the whole US Army.

In this age of the potential for instant global annihilation, one wonders what the old cavalryman knew. Polo and horseback riding have very recently become growth sports in America, and are increasing at a phenomenal rate. Horse races and rodeos, of course, are perennial favorites, and the cavalry, regardless of what form it takes, is still called the cavalry. But if numbers have any significance, one must wonder what some recent statistics tell us about our faithful steeds.

In 1920 there were upward of 25 million horses in the United States; in 1929 there were 12 million, and in the 1950s, only three million. But in 1971 the American horse population rose to 6.2 million, and in 1983 to 8.3 million. What does it mean? Perhaps man is not entirely prepared to relinquish control to the machines he has created, or has begun in earnest to learn how to control them. One way or another, the mobility of the fighting man will continue to be necessary, and the cavalry will continue to exist.

Main picture: *US Army M-1 Abrams tanks make their European Field Training debut during NATO exercises 'Reforger 82.'*

Top: *The newly developed M-2 Bradley Fighting Vehicle, demonstrated here at Fort Benning, Georgia, improves cavalry units, mobility, security and reconnaissance potential.*

Right: *A head-on view of the new M-1 Abrams during recent NATO exercises.*

Right: *The AH-64 Apache Advance Attack Helicopter is an anti-tank weapon designed to fly by day or by night. A 30mm chain gun is mounted in the turret, and Hellfire missiles complete the armaments complement.*

Below left: *US Army Air Assault School trainees running with their weapons during a physical training session.*

Below right: *The 'winged horse' has a secure place in the US Army of the future for missions in the cavalry tradition of speed, skill and surprise.*

Index

Page numbers in italics refer to illustrations.

Picture Credits
American Graphic Systems: 32–3 (below), 33, 131, 132 (left), 137 (top right & below), 142 (right).
Bibliothèque Nationale, Paris: 10 (bottom), 11 (bottom).
Bison Picture Library: 26 (top), 67 (below), 79 (both), 161, 171 (below).
Bodleian Library, Oxford: 11 (top, center), 12 (below, both).
British Museum Library Board: 10 (center), 11 (left & top right).
Anne S K Brown Military Collection, Brown University Library: 30 (top), 31 (both), 35 (above), 36 (above), 38-9 (all), 49 (below), 64, 65 (below), 66-7 (above), 66 (below), 70-71, 72-3, 74-5, 114-15, 118 (all), 119 (both), 126-7 (above), 148-9.
California State Library: 48-9.
Chicago Historical Society: 15.
Colorado Historical Society: 122.
Corcoran Gallery of Art, Washington, DC: 45 (below).
Currier and Ives: 78 (top).
Mary Evans Picture Library: 9 (below).
Harper's Weekly: 92 (above).
Imperial War Museum, London: 180 (center).
H W Koch Collection: 9 (above).
Eric Lessing: 10 (top).
Library of Congress: 14 (below), 16-17, 20, 24-5, 37 (below), 46 (below), 48 (left), 52 (top), 54-5, 57 (below), 58-9 (both), 60-61 (above), 61 (below), 62 (both), 63, 67 (above), 68, 68-9 (above), 69, 70 (left), 73 (below), 82-3, 84, 86

(top), 87, 88-9, 90 (left), 90-91, 94-5, 97, 98-9 (above), 100, 101 (above), 102-03, 104-05 (above), 105, 107 (above), 108, 110-11, 112-13 (all), 116 (right), 125 (above), 128 (below), 129 (below), 132-3, 138, 140-41 (below), 142 (left), 143 (both), 150 (above), 151 (above), 153 (above), 155 (left, both), 157, 162-3, 164 (top), 165, 168, 169 (top), 174, 175 (both).
Metropolitan Museum of Art, New York, New York: 17 (right).
Elizabeth Myles Montgomery: 129 (top).
Museum of the City of New York: 27.
National Archives: 29 (below), 44-5 (above), 117 (inset), 120-21, 124 (above), 125 (below), 128 (above), 130, 134 (both), 136 (left), 136-7, 141 (top), 144-5 (both), 152-3 (main picture), 158, 159 (below), 161 (top).
National Museum of American Art: 26 (below).
National Portrait Gallery, Smithsonian Institution; on loan from the National Museum of American Art: 26 (below).
National Museum of American Art, Smithsonian Institution: 44 (below).
Peter Newark's Historical Pictures: 8, 12 (top), 13 (left, both), 21 (both), 28 (below), 65 (top), 76 (both), 77.
Peter Newark's Western Americana: 13 (right), 16 (left), 19 (below), 23 (below), 32-3 (above), 34, 34-5, 36, 37 (above), 42, 43 (both), 46 (above), 46-7, 52 (below), 53, 56 (left), 56-7, 60 (below), 80 (all), 85 (both), 92-3, 96 (both), 99 (below), 101 (below), 104 (below), 107 (below), 109 (both), 117 (main picture), 123 (both), 124

(below), 126 (left, both), 126-7 (below), 127 (right, both), 140 (top), 146-7 (main picture), 151 (below), 152 (above), 155 (top right), 160, 162 (left), 170, 173 (top), 180 (top).
The New York Historical Society, New York City: 28-9, 30 (below left).
New York Public Library Picture Collection: 14 (top), 18, 19 (above), 81.
Smithsonian Institution, National Anthropological Archives: 133 (below), 135, 139 (below), 144 (below), 146 (left).
South Dakota State Historical Society: 139 (top), 147 (inset).
US Army Photo: 169 (below), 171 (top), 176 (both), 178 (both), 178-9.
US Cavalry Museum, Fort Riley, Kansas: 150 (below), 164 (below), 172 (top), 172-3.
US Defense Department: 41 (inset), 166-7, 177 (both), 178-9 (inset), 179 (top), 181 (both), 183 (top), 185 (top), 185 (below right), 188-9.
US Navy, Naval Photographic Center: 40-41, 86 (below), 106, 154, 156 (left), 156 (right), 159 (top).
Valley Forge Historical Society: 6-7.
Yale University Art Gallery, Joseph Szaszfai photo: 22-3.

Acknowledgments
The publisher would like to thank the following people who have helped in the preparation of this book: Michael Rose, who designed it; Robin Langley Sommer, who edited it; Mary R Raho, who did the picture research; and Florence Norton, who prepared the index.